A Testimony of Love and Devotion

My Life Journey with Paramahansa Yogananda

by Mary Peck Stockton

Tamaltree Books
Portland, Oregon

A Testimony of Love and Devotion
My Life Journey with Paramahansa Yogananda

Copyright © 2001 by Mary Peck Stockton

Printed in the United States of America
Second printing June 2001
9 8 7 6 5 4 3 2 1

ISBN 0-9709709-3-5

Published by Tamaltree Books
P.O. Box 80764
Portland, Oregon 97280

Dedication

This book is dedicated to God, Christ, and my

Guru, Paramahansa Yogananda, who took me

on a lifelong journey that culminated in

freedom and peace. It is also dedicated to Sri

Daya Mata, our beloved president of Self-

Realization Fellowship (SRF), whose eternal

friendship and wisdom are guiding me through

my earthly trials and spiritual growth. And

with special love and thanks to my mother who

brought me to this path.

TABLE OF CONTENTS

- ✺ Memories of attending services conducted by
  Paramahansa Yogananda.
- ✺ Impressions of his appearance and manner
  while giving lectures.
- ✺ His influence and guidance in my life.
- ✺ SRF churches in the early days.

- ✺ Master's cover of protection during childhood
  dangers from threats of violence.
- ✺ His continuing words of comfort and protective
  cover through difficult times and throughout
  all my life.
- ✺ His protection over my brother and mother.

- ✺ Master's wise guidance in making fateful
  decisions.
- ✺ His enduring words of help throughout my
  professional career.
- ✺ A visit with Master in his quarters in Los Angeles.
- ✺ His guidance providing help in times of need.

FOREWORD

by
Radhika Swamy
SRF Devotee, Chennai, India
formerly of New Delhi
December 2000

Mary Peck Stockton

This book is Mary Stockton's chronicle of her deep faith in and devotion to her Guru, Paramahansa Yogananda. It gives encouragement and hope to those whose souls are going through "the dark night." Those hearts bewildered with trials will find a succor in the words of Mary—words of one who lived during Master's time, of one who has seen him and conversed with him and, above all, one who has trod the path that her Guru showed her with faith, fearlessness, and total surrender.

In this book Mary describes the awe she felt for this ochre-clad preacher with long hair and glowing eyes! Never did she dare look up into his eyes; with eyes downcast she would always manage to look at his shoes! Little did she then, as a child, know what a guru is and what an important role he was to play in her life! She would notice that he brought out some "crumpled dollar notes" to give to her mother. This act of compassion shaped her life of giving freely to others.

Master's help was always forthcoming. A lot of discipline, too, came her way, to help in weeding out unwanted qualities. Mary writes about the episode when Master asked her to sing for no less a personage than Amelita Galli-Curci! Humility was taught to her that day.

Several years ago, Mary's article entitled "Never-Ending Blessings" was published in one of the SRF magazines. Here she wrote about her supernatural experience of 1983, when Master took her by the hand and led her to the astral realms. The article's vivid descriptions and the sincerity of her words have given a great deal of hope to many who have read it. Mary explains that prayers are of substance and that each prayer floated up in the form of a feather to uphold her. She was told to pass along the message of forgiveness, too. The astral world experience is described in detail in this book.

In his commentary on the *Bhagavad Gita*, Master talks about fearlessness. To be fit for discipline, a devotee has got to be fearless. Mary Stockton is indeed a shining example of fearlessness! Those who know her can vouch for this. Her own life is a testimony of her unshakeable faith in her Guru. From that kind of faith came fearlessness.

Mary has been through the worst kind of life-threatening illnesses, but she always emerged victorious. She has undergone fourteen major surgeries, has been paralyzed and a victim of severe accidents, but Satan could never pull her down, as she always clung to God. She writes in vivid detail about some of her seemingly insurmountable difficulties and how she triumphed over all of them. Master's help and the courage and strength she acquired through her deep attunement to him made the impossible, possible. Mary speaks and writes with the conviction of one who has seen the power of Master, and one who has received his blessings.

David, her husband, has been a bulwark, always there for Mary, steadily and silently helping her through the tests and trials. He has been of yeoman service in helping her prepare this book.

May this book act as a source of strength and succor to all those who are heavily burdened with suffering as they march on toward their goal—Self-Realization!

Jai Guru!

Mary Peck Stockton

FOREWORD
by
Paul Gorsuch
SRF Devotee
Seattle, Washington
December 2000

Mary Peck Stockton

The chelas of Paramahansa Yogananda have been blessed with a wealth of material from their Guru. Rare among avatars, the great Master left volumes of His teachings for the ages. The love and discipline of a great Master are also illustrated in the stories of His direct disciples. Mary Stockton's book shares some stories from a soul that had the privilege to know the great Master while He graced this world in a physical form. And yet, her writings are not simply tales from the past. Her words show the eternal promise of a true Guru—One who guides and protects His dear ones, no matter where the Guru and disciple reside.

In a letter to another cherished disciple over 50 years ago, the great Master stated that a smooth life was not a victorious life. The words in Mary's book do not describe a smooth life. These pages describe and illustrate something more lasting and substantial. They testify to the eternal love and protection of a Master. The stories within also show something very important for all to realize: It is not necessary to have known the Guru while He was in the body. The love and protection of such a One are not limited by the circumstances of time and place.

In the years I have known the author, I was occasionally

privileged to see some of these laws of Divine Love in action. There were times when I knew that she was being tested with serious physical illness. At such times, there was almost always a perceptible glow around her form. It was as if one was being shown the relative importance of the body and the soul. Physical illness could not diminish the light of her soul though the body was suffering. Through attunement with her Guru, Mary was able to tune in with His Omnipresent help and get through another test of faith.

This demonstration of love also contains one of the greatest values in reading stories about a Guru. A disciple does not have to be perfect to be loved by their Guru. Anyone who can relate to that love can add a page of experience to that person's book of devotion. May all that read these pages feel the experiences of the author translated into their own heartfelt connection with the Divine.

Acknowledgements

Mary Peck Stockton

∾

This book would never have been written without constant requests from many members of SRF who repeatedly asked to know more of Paramahansa Yogananda through my experiences with him.

As a direct answer to prayer, we were blessed to be sent a family from India that opened the world of love between us and the homeland of our beloved Guru. These beautiful souls were ever encouraging and demonstrating Master's infinite universal love. Mr. Swamy, Radhika, and Shekhar Swamy became our ambassadors of good will from New Delhi, India. Their encouragement to write this book made me realize I could achieve universal understanding of my blessed experiences.

In Seattle, Washington many wonderful souls who were constantly encouraging and praying for me through some difficult tests urged me to write of the experiences for others, so that they would not be lost to future devotees. Paul Gorsuch, one of the Seattle devotees, became another "son" to me with love, help, and encouragement. His prayers were so strong that they were as "healing feathers" under my wing.

In Portland, Oregon when it was "time" to write this book and I needed professional direction, Master, in answer to prayer, provided the very capable and talented writer-teacher, Bill Johnson. He gave specific instruction and encouragement to complete my assigned task. His own book, *A Story Is a Promise*, is dedicated to our mutual Guru.

Elizabeth Waldman Frazier, also, called at the right time as she responded to the call from Master in meditation. She aided in the book's progress with her editing experience, typing, and manuscript preparation skills. Her loyal enthusiasm and dedication to help us with this book is an example of Master's love. In the exchange of time and words we have developed a deep friendship.

Sri Daya Mata has been a constant and ever sustaining guide and friend throughout the years. Her letters of encouragement, love, and teachings have helped me grow in wisdom, spirit and truth.

Not the least, but closest to my heart, is my husband David, who listened, typed, discussed, and helped me produce this book from the beginning. He spent many hours at his computer to bring you my journey through life, sharing the blessings given me by Paramahansa Yogananda.

My children—Peter, Mary, Troy, Kim, Hannah—have been most supportive of this effort.

My thanks to God, Paramahansa Yogananda, and Sri Daya Mata for giving me the extended time and energy to make this book happen.

Introduction

∾

I am one who was blessed to know Paramahansa Yogananda in person. I will take you through my journal of experiences to show he is ever alive in spirit, and how he has blessed my life. My story speaks to you who are chosen to be householders ... as am I. It is a story of one who has lived fully in this world and has been saved by the spiritual guidance of my Guru.

Who was this man of God? Not an elusive, unreachable figure, but one of universal love and acceptance. This man, the epitome of excellence, remains with me forever in our spiritual communion. As you read these words, I will lead you through my journey with him.

My purpose in writing this book is to answer the questions from the many who have inquired about my early years' experiences living in the presence of Paramahansa Yogananda, and how his teachings have supported me throughout all my life. Since writing a previously published magazine article about my memories, many recollections have returned to me that could not be included in that short article. Many years have gone by, but every memory, movement, expression, and word of wisdom I recall by our beloved Guru is cherished in my heart; these are offered to you for greater understanding of this beautiful soul.

With this purpose in mind, I offer you that which I experienced being in his actual presence from 1932 to 1950. Since I last saw him in 1950, his teachings, wisdom, and blessings have continued to guide and sustain me through all the years up to the present day.

My intention is to describe Master as best I can, so those that did not know him in the body may get a glimpse of him through my eyes. I trust the experiences related give an honest measure of his blessings, his teachings, and his manner, as well as the guidance and protection that have molded and shaped my life.

His spirit remains with me to this day. It is even stronger than when I had the blessings of his bodily presence. His unceasing blessings have guided, protected, and urged me on toward God. I am, and always will be, loyal to my chosen path of Self-Realization Fellowship (SRF).

You must understand that I am not more special than each of you, dear reader. When you choose Paramahansa Yogananda as your Guru, you are *his*, just as I am. Even though it was surely special to know Master in the body, you—through the lessons and meditations—may know him in the spirit. He is always near. He is ever with those who have accepted him in their hearts, minds, and souls as their own beloved Guru/teacher. I am reminded that on my last visit with Sri Daya Mata, she conveyed the message that all can receive communion in spirit with our Guru through meditative prayer.

The chapter on guidance is a collection of thoughts from Master's teachings in the hope that you open your heart and mind to receive intuition leading to your own inner guidance. The list of short, random statements in the chapter, "Whispers from Master," was recorded on scraps of paper saved over a period of twenty-five years. These intuitive thoughts came to guide me in answer to prayers. The majority were given me during the quiet late night and early morning hours. I include them so that one or more may spark a thought to comfort, guide, or give an instruction to you at an opportune time of need.

Through the years my total respect and friendship for Sri Daya Mata has lifted my consciousness of Master, and has clarified the meaning of his teachings. The chapter about Sri Daya Mata is to share the love and respect I dearly hold for her. She has been a cherished friend throughout these years, and is an inspiration in my life.

The poems and prayers chapter has been included to speak of my love for God, and to ask for His presence and intervention in personal and worldly matters.

Paramahansa Yogananda, as my God-illumined Guru, is my spiritual teacher. He is one who has realized God. He serves to lead me on my inward journey toward Divine realization through teachings handed down from God, through Jesus Christ, God-realized masters, and saints. These teachings uplift my soul through prayer and meditation so that I may attain peace and universal love.

The writings in this book are my impressions alone. No attempt has been made to copy any publications of Self-Realization Fellowship (SRF). Rather, these personal writings relate the blessings I received from Master, as I lived them. Now, in my final years, is the time to pass on these experiences. I offer these to you with my deepest sincerity and love.

May his peace and love be ever yours.

CHAPTER ONE

Living Memories of
Paramahansa Yogananda

When I was about seven years old, the *San Diego Union* newspaper carried an article that drew my mother's attention. It told of a visiting lecturer from India—his name was Swami Yogananda. At that time—in 1931—the title of Paramahansa had not yet been bestowed on him. My mother was compelled to attend that lecture. She was transformed by his words of spiritual hope and encouragement.

Following his lecture, he received individuals who came forth to meet him. My mother went to shake his hand and, hopefully, to receive a blessing. He asked her to step aside and wait for him until after he'd greeted other people from the audience. When he had finished, he approached my mother.

They had a short conversation and, at the end, he asked her to follow his teachings. She had told him of our violent home situation with my father, and that she was the mother of two young children. She was not free at that time to join the organization in his service; however, she did promise to study his lessons. She said she would join his group of disciples when the opportunity arose. This opportunity came and was fulfilled in 1950.

My mother attended Master's meetings whenever she

could. After one of the lectures, she asked if he would heal a large boil on her leg. She came home very excited and told us of the instantaneous healing she had received.

More and more she studied Master's materials and meditated. I never questioned what my mother was doing when she stayed quietly in her room for such long periods of time. In those days, children were to be seen and not heard. We did observe that my mother was increasingly calm. Her attitude toward others became more accepting and kind.

So that you can understand my background, I should explain to you some of my mother's history. She was born in Russia into a family that lived in a small farming village. My grandfather immigrated to Philadelphia where he worked to be able to send money to Russia in order to bring his young wife and family to America. My mother, at the time of her arrival on Ellis Island in 1906, was one year old. She was educated in the Philadelphia public schools.

Because times were so difficult for this family in America, my mother was compelled to leave school to work at a succession of menial jobs. She was forced to contribute her earnings to help support her family.

When she was sixteen, my mother met and married my father, nine years her elder. He was a sailor and had experiences that intrigued my mother in the light of her limited background. Naval duty transferred my father to San Diego. The beauty of that city so fascinated my mother that she vowed never to leave the area.

By the time she was nineteen, my mother had given birth to my brother and me. Our family life was very difficult, which led to my mother's need to find spiritual sustenance.

As I have previously stated, my mother met Master in San Diego. He inspired her to become the best person she could be. To my mother this meant completing the schooling she had been forced to abandon many years previous to her attendance in Master's classes. She completed her grade school training, then went on to attend adult high school at night. Upon graduation, she had achieved more education than anyone else in her family, which pleased Master.

My brother and I benefited from my mother's zeal for schooling. She educated my brother and me by reading us the great books of classical literature. She drove us to an isolated part of San Diego, parked the car, and read to her captured audience many times. We received an education beyond our years.

I was, also, allowed to attend adult high school with her when I was about eleven years old. I learned many valuable lessons that prepared me for an early entry to college. Both my brother and I went on through college to obtain graduate degrees. His was preparation through naval studies that allowed him to advance his rank in the navy. My education led me through the paths of psychology, education, and administration as my life's work.

While I was still attending undergraduate school in San Diego, I urged my mother to further her studies. We took college classes together as a challenge to one another and enjoyed the uplifting social life on campus. After I graduated, my mother stayed on to complete her BA degree in education.

I returned home from graduate school at the University of Southern California to proudly congratulate my mother upon her graduation from San Diego State College. Master's influence had not only helped her, but his guidance led my brother and me to achieve our best. Had she not met Master, where would her life have led … and my brother's and mine?

Now—returning to my recollections of Master's presence in my life—the exact year of my brother's and my personal introduction to the services given by Swami Yogananda eludes my memory. I was curious why we went to a church where the "minister" wore an orange robe and had hair longer than mine! My brother and I had attended Sunday school at a neighboring Lutheran church in San Diego. Now we began attending lectures by Swami Yogananda. This was an experience very different from our previous church attendance. Master would tell his congregation repeatedly that he was not preaching a sermon, but that he was teaching us how to know God.

When we were in his presence, I noted the calmness and peace that surrounded Master. This was so different than being around my father. I felt safe in the aura and spirit of Master's presence and I was always in awe of him.

Paramahansaji wore an orange robe over dark pants that

extended down to his shoe tops. His shoes were black and kept shining and new looking. His dark hair, very wavy, fell to his shoulders and beyond. He had a habit of brushing his hair back with a graceful sweep of his hand. His skin was colored a light brown and his complexion was clear and smooth. His ever-present ochre robe was fixed at the shoulder with a Self-Realization Fellowship (SRF) lotus pin. Often, the soft material of his robe would slide out of place and he would patiently return it to its original position.

Like a warm, protective ocean, Master's aura exuded love, peace, and calm. He was kingly in his carriage and always stood straight. This made me think he was taller than his actual height. I was impressed from the moment I first saw him with how his bearing spoke silently of courage and love.

Although Master's attitude was one of decorum, he had a delightful sense of humor and enjoyed laughing with his devotees. During most of his Sunday lectures, he introduced humor and would laugh, hale and hearty, right along with his delighted listeners. At times, during his lectures, he questioned the audience with a twinkle in his eye, and, with a slight smile, asked if anyone could guess how old he was. The answers from the audience produced an amazing span of years. He would laugh and say that he never would tell us how old he was. Truly, his countenance remained youthful throughout the years.

Master's voice—well modulated—rose and fell in pitch and decibels to express the internal feelings he projected. To capture the full attention of his listeners, his voice ranged from whispered phrases to a great booming volume. It always commanded attention and, no doubt, kept the listeners interested. He preceded his lectures by asking if we were awake and ready, and we were required to affirm his inquiry. He wanted no one sleeping mentally while he offered God's precious gems of wisdom. I remember times when he was speaking, Master's eyes became still and his speech would fade off into silence.

He said he was gazing at the vision of the beloved Lord. He broke his silence to tell us that Christ himself was with us here and was blessing us. A feeling of joy and peace filled my heart that remained with me for a long time following the services.

Master always urged us to pray for understanding. He told us that with understanding in your heart you would be able to adjust to anyone or any situation. Keep that instruction in mind as you nurture and raise your children and as you interact with others. Followed correctly and sincerely, our Guru's lessons embrace every physical, emotional, and spiritual need. Follow the guidance gleaned through your meditation; make your goal to be a God-like person living for God alone.

In my youth, I often saw a lovely young woman efficiently and busily taking notes at Master's lectures. Quietly serene, she went about her tasks with obvious joy serving her Guru. She became my teen idol—one whom I tried to emulate. This

Mary Peck Stockton

person was Miss Faye Wright, who is now known as Sri Daya Mata, our beloved president.

Often, Master would sweetly refer to his mother. He reverently told us of her beautiful eyes and countenance. He spoke in tones low and loving, making you feel as though you had met her. His despair at losing her was conveyed as he told us of the search for her loving eyes after she had left the body, eyes that were found once again in meditation—the comforting eyes of his Mother God.

Because of my strict upbringing, I was a very shy, controlled child and my eyes were most often focused downward. Instead of looking into Master's face, my gaze traveled down to his feet and observed his black laced shoes. When I visited Encinitas some sixty years later, I saw his shoes displayed under the bed in his bedroom at the Hermitage. It filled me so full of memories it touched my heart, and I began to cry as I felt overwhelming love emanating from that room. I quietly said to his presence, "Master, I'm home."

My mother took us to services at Encinitas until the temple in San Diego was acquired. We then began to attend weekly services in San Diego. Master would travel down from the north to bless us with his presence. While attending church, I noticed that Master seemed to be studying me. He watched me for quite awhile, but said nothing. I thought, because of my strict upbringing, that I'd done something wrong, and that I was in for some kind of correction.

Years later, I questioned Daya Mata why this occurred.

She told me that Master had recognized me from the many times I'd been with him in past incarnations. Of course, I was not advanced enough to realize this, but he certainly continued to watch my spiritual growth throughout the ensuing years.

We occasionally returned to Encinitas to enjoy the services there. Master had planned, designed, and overseen the actual building of the first beautiful Golden Lotus Temple of All Religions that sat on the cliffs in Encinitas overlooking the ocean. Tinted glass windows rose to the ceiling and spanned the entire west wall. This gave a magnificent view of the sea below.

Master conducted services sitting to the audience's right as we faced him. He played the harmonium, rendering Eastern music unfamiliar to my classically trained ear. Therefore, I had some difficulty learning the chants he offered to us. One favorite song ending the service was his adaptation of "The Battle Hymn of the Republic." He sang it with such gusto that most listeners were inspired to join him loudly and strongly because they were familiar with that tune. His energy flowed forth as he emphasized the "glory" and "hallelujah" words that evoked full attention and response from his audience. His mighty voice boomed forth as strong and audibly as the ocean that was visible through the large windows in back of him. I was aware of his deep sincerity, and his audience responded to it, as we were gathered up into the power and presence evident in the room.

Mary Peck Stockton

Often during the meditation portion of the service he became very quiet for a long time. Then, in a rapture-filled soft voice, he told us that Christ was here in the room with us, and that we were being blessed as he saw us bathed in a great light. I recognized that overwhelming feeling as the one I had felt when I was three years old. Although I did not understand the significance at that time, I recall that blessing even now and it touches my heart and comforts me.

During construction of the first Golden Lotus Temple, Master seemed very happy. He had commissioned workers in India to form and create its golden lotus as well as those that presently adorn the entry to the Encinitas grounds. He reported on their progress from time to time and told us of the procedures necessary to lay the gold leaf on them. What a delicate task to assemble the lotuses; how beautiful the result! A very happy Master announced their arrival after a year's work. He received them with great joy and love, and certainly not a small amount of gratitude for the workers in India who produced them.

A landslide destroyed the beautiful temple because of the sea-pounded, weakened cliffs. We were all shocked and dismayed. Fortunately, it did not occur at a time when the temple was occupied. Master, though disappointed, took everything in his stride. He was a great role model of steadiness and calm—necessary for a true Yogi through both adversity and joy.

Master honored and helped all kinds of people. A variety of people stood in line in order to pay homage to him. Obviously wealthy individuals wearing expensive clothing, as well as people representing the middle class and poor waited to receive his blessings. Some were crippled and leaned on canes as they waited patiently in line to receive his love, healing, and guidance. Because of my youth, I questioned why so many "different" people yearned to see him. It was a lifetime lesson for me to see his equal treatment of everyone. He treated all with the same warmth and compassion. He paid sincere attention to the needs individuals presented to him.

As far as I can remember, the Worldwide Healing Services were conducted as part of the regular church service. During the services Master explained the value of group prayer to us as we joined together to extend our arms and chant Aum. Following some services, Master would see individuals regarding their need for healing. He would give them guidance in private. I was sensitive to the great vibrations that came from this procedure. Master urged us all to follow his instructions and prayers in the *Scientific Healing Affirmations* to receive help for individual needs.

I was not aware of special services for healing that Master might have held. My mother did not share this information with me.

As my life unfolded, I became more and more involved with helping people of all circumstances. My assignments and career opportunities led me to deal with those from all segments of our society, as well as some from foreign lands. I worked with handicapped children and adults and later helped adults fulfill their lifetime ambitions at the college level. A necessary ingredient in dealing with these differing situations was the balanced approach that Master taught. As a result of his mentorship, my eyes were opened to the true body, soul, and material needs of the people to whom I was sent in my work.

When I was a child, a demonstration of Master's generosity was displayed one Sunday in Encinitas. My mother went forward to shake Master's hand. She told him we had very little money for food. My heart was touched as I saw the dear saint reach into his pocket, extend his hand, and press some crumpled paper money into my mother's hand. Never before had I seen such an immediate display of active caring.

At that time, the India Café was opened to the public. I was quite curious about the fare and thought I'd like to try the food made as the East Indians would prepare it. I expressed my curiosity and desire to sample these dishes to my mother. I was hopeful that Master's monetary gift could buy us a taste of that unfamiliar food. She did not assuage my curiosity. Instead, after services, she drove my brother and me to a small drug store fountain in Del Mar, a short distance from Encinitas. That particular fountain sold large, juicy hamburgers that would fill us at a price we could better afford. Needless to say, we did not follow the yogi example of proper eating!

Often after church services in Encinitas, Master would entertain a group of visitors in the Hermitage dining room. He also took them to the India Café. I longed to be on his guest list, but a pre-teen would have been quite out of place with the distinguished guests. I was very aware of those lucky ones who were included in these luncheons, and only wished that, some day, I could be one of them. I never did make it to his table in this life, but I have feasted mightily at his spiritual table.

One vivid memory of Encinitas that I hold dear was seeing Master and Rajarsi Janakananda (Mr. James Lynn) emerge from their meditation on the beach below the Hermitage. Hand-in-hand, they would practically skip across campus in obvious joy retained from meditation. The radiance emanating from their faces I shall never forget! Their spiritual love was so all-encompassing. God's presence was visible in their faces, and an aura of peace and joy was felt as they passed by. At that time, I wondered if I could ever find that sublime feeling; if I could ever find that happiness.

Sister Gyanamata seemed always to be present in Encinitas. She kept quietly busy completing tasks for Master. Her countenance was one of serene beauty. Childish as I was, I thought, "How clean she looks!" Her garb was that of a nun and her head was covered with a pure white cloth that touched her shoulders. She seemed to speak very little and went about her tasks in concentrated silence. Master,

Mary Peck Stockton

when he wrote of her passing, referred to her as a saint. She was so very loyal, true, and helpful to Master through the years.

Dr. and Mrs. Lewis were frequent visitors to Encinitas, and they were amongst those "lucky ones" who were invited to lunch with Master. Later, when the San Diego Center had been purchased and completed, Doctor Lewis took over responsibility for the services when Master was away. I remember, at those times, being disappointed that Master was not with us, but Doctor Lewis certainly served us well; he was congenial and thorough in his presentations. Later, Doctor Lloyd Kennell joined the ministerial staff in San Diego and conducted services there.

What a joy it was when Master returned to San Diego after one of his absences! The picture of Master standing in front of the San Diego Church that was printed in the SRF magazine was taken at the time we were in attendance. I felt honored to be there to watch the photographer and Master getting just the "right pose" that would be used later. I have saved the SRF magazines that reproduced that particular pose.

One Sunday, Master announced that we in the congregation were invited to visit the Hermitage in Encinitas for a tour of the grounds and Master's quarters. We happily traveled to Encinitas. I was impressed with the great peace felt in each room as we were escorted throughout the building. Master took great pleasure in showing us treasures that he had brought from India, as he guided us through his living room. The rooms emanated the pleasant odor of sandalwood, both from the furniture constructed of that wood and, also, the burning incense; the scent to this day makes me feel at "home." Master was our delightful "tour guide." He seemed quite happy to share his beloved Hermitage with his visitors.

When I was twelve and my brother fourteen, my mother decided that we *must* learn to drive. My brother, of course, was delighted! He got along very well with things mechanical. I, on the other hand, do *not* like machinery. So I balked at the thought.

Mother was a tough taskmaster. She would never allow the word "no" to escape my lips.

She had requested that my father give her a car of her own because she was not allowed to touch *his* new DeSoto. Reluctantly, he provided my mother with a 1912 Buick. This was in 1936. So our saga of driving lessons began. Mother took my brother and me to the outskirts of San Diego in the roughest terrain she could find. There, she "mapped out" a driving course that would call for anyone's superior driving skills.

Mother instructed each of us how to shift and use the pedals. I absolutely hated the task she was forcing me to learn. Tears streamed down my face as I clutched the heavy steering wheel with both hands. I jerked and jerked us through lesson after lesson and finally learned how to handle

Mary Peck Stockton

the monster.

It became imperative that I had driving skills because I was expected to supplement our family income. The persistence and self-control I learned from those terrible driving lessons helped me to face many future trials with determination.

The state of California issued me a special license to drive because of family hardship. I was twelve when I took my first job, delivering goods and medicines for a local drugstore. Fortunately, a more updated car than ours was furnished, so I got to my destinations quite well.

As is true of all challenges in life, the hard lessons paid off. All my future employment required that I travel many, many miles.

In 1938 Master announced that Easter services would be held outdoors on the lawn of the Encinitas hermitage. Since we lived in San Diego, we were aware that we would have to hurry to be on time. I remember how sleepy I was as my mother prodded my brother and me to get dressed. I was fourteen at the time, and my brother was sixteen. Neither of us felt like hurrying out of our warm beds, but my mother's insistence moved us to "get going."

We often were late to services in Encinitas because of the distance we needed to travel. When we arrived that Easter, every seat was taken. Master was standing on the cliff overlooking the sea. A slight breeze gently moved his robe and the scene made a memorable picture.

That picture has often been printed in the SRF magazine. It shows Master facing the sea, with the visitors seated in the background. There were a few of us standing in back of the people who were seated, and centered amongst them are my mother, brother, and me. At least we "stood out" in the crowd of attendees.

Sixty-one years later, I returned to stand on the very spot I stood on that wonderful morning. My husband took my picture as I recalled the thrill of that beautiful Easter service on the very same ground, to which, by the grace of God, I'd been allowed to return.

My mother saved a vast amount of SRF publications and letters, which I discovered upon her death in 1995. In my mother's materials, I came across an item that told me of the radio broadcasts Master presented in order to bring spiritual education to all. She had inscribed "KGN" on the announcement. I believe this was a Los Angeles radio station at that time. He certainly used every opportunity to inform the public about his spiritual message brought to us from India.

An item my mother had saved, gleaned from materials advertised in the SRF magazine, was a psychological profile that I used as a case study guide in my professional work. It was an outline to help understand the physical, environmental, and emotional state of the child or adult being studied. It was so complete and thorough that I did not need to change it. Its use gave me a complete overview of the individual and his needs.

Healing and guidance interviews with devotees were a regular part of the spiritual service Master offered in the early days, and many visitors came from all parts of the world to see him. Because of the ever-increasing volume of his writing activities, Master concentrated on this work and saw fewer devotees as time passed. Toward the end of his life, he was able to see only a few individuals.

He kept up with many devotees through correspondence, and Mother and I were amongst the very fortunate to receive his letters of guidance and encouragement. I still possess letters that end with the words, "Unceasing Blessings." All my life I have been blessed with these unceasing blessings. Once you are centered in God's love, unceasing blessings will be yours forever.

While attending Sunday services in all the centers, I was particularly impressed with the quality of people I met there. They were so sincere, loving, and intelligent. Master's audiences included people from all steps of life. As I became acquainted and interacted with many of his devotees, I was inspired to emulate them in order to be of service to God. I find the same spirit in today's devotees that I admired in my youth.

Master loved music and he invited famous musicians from places near and far to visit him. Korla Pandet, a very popular organist in Los Angeles, gave special performances and other East Indian musicians brought their instruments to participate in the kirtans held at headquarters. These were world-renowned musicians only too happy to play for him and his appreciative friends. Master also enjoyed playing his harmonium to the accompaniment of drums and other instruments. His entire being seemed to become one with the music as he sang and swayed to the rhythms of his beloved India. He told us that "The Song of India" was one of his favorite musical pieces and that, also, he enjoyed "The Blue Danube" because of its lovely descriptive melody.

Master spoke and sang with a well-modulated, dramatically expressive voice. The effect upon the listeners was as though we had all been embraced with his spirit. The accompaniment from his harmonium rose and fell with the soul expression of his voice. If you, as part of the audience, did not join in the soulful renditions with gusto, he would repeatedly urge, "louder" until all were one with him in glorious sound.

Madame Galli-Curci, a famous diva of the Metropolitan Opera, was a devotee and close friend of Master. She would often attend services at the San Diego church. My burning life's ambition from the age of five was to be an opera singer. God had graced me with a nice singing voice, and I felt that life would not be worth living if I didn't get to sing professionally. I was in my early teens and was certainly bitten by the performance "bug."

One Sunday, Master asked me to sing at the service. I said to myself, This will be a piece of cake. I had been singing in public and professionally for many years so this request did not disturb me. When the time came for the service to begin, I was directed to a chair on the dais to the right of Master. That day, Madame Galli-Curci, the great opera diva, was seated in the audience about three or four rows from the front. Before the service began, Master reminded me to sing only for God. I thought surely I was going to do just that.

As the service began, while we were meditating, Master asked me if I saw Sri Yukteswarji. I replied, "No, but I see the bald guru with the full face." Paramahansaji seemed to be very surprised at the vision I had been given. I had been blessed with a vision of Lahiri Mahasaya! Master said nothing further to me. Perhaps that vision was to foretell my spiritual path as a householder—the same path Lahiri Mahasaya had followed.

The time came for me to stand up and sing. I looked at the audience, and Master's admonition to sing only for God quickly escaped me, as I sought to impress the listeners. Replacing Master's reminder to me was the possibility that I might be "discovered." In my youthful ignorance, I was envisioning a rise to stardom! I nodded to the accompanist to begin, then opened my mouth and waited for the first dulcet tone to be forthcoming.

What came out astonished me—I sounded like a croaking frog! None of the vocal tricks I'd learned to clear my throat worked. I tried to complete the disastrous performance to no avail. I sat down silent and dejected. Master said nothing and the service continued. Needless to say, Madame Galli-Curci did not rush up after the service to congratulate me. Nor was there an offer for stardom!

Years later, while reading Master's writings about the fellow who was demonstrating hatha yoga postures with his ego in the fore, a big light exploded in my mind as I recalled my disastrous performance. The young man, as he flexed his muscles to impress the audience, was rendered incapable of completing his now hapless performance. I started to laugh as the memory of my performance rushed back to me. Master taught this young man and me not to assuage our egos in attempts to be appreciated for our efforts, but rather to give God all the credit for our talents. That was a hard lesson in humility for a young girl to learn, yet one I shall never forget. You might be interested to know that I did recover my singing ability well enough to become a professional singer. The money I earned from singing helped pay my way through college. Every experience has its purpose and is written into God's scenario for each of us.

A more serious hard lesson for me to learn was given me when I was in college. I had my first surgical experience, with death as a possible outcome. It became necessary for me to have a double mastectomy. Surgical knowledge and procedures in the 1940's were more primitive than they are today in 2001. I was only eighteen years old and my recovery became very much in doubt. The doctor who performed my surgery proved to be quite incompetent. Therefore, my brush with death was very real.

My mother asked for prayers and support from Master and they were forthcoming. Most young women, I feel, would be devastated by the physical loss, but through God's and Master's grace, it became a test of my true being. I sought to develop my soul and not to focus on my body. My character then turned more spiritual, for which I am extremely grateful.

While I was in graduate school, I sang in many places in order to pay my tuition at the University of Southern California. I now had to make a definite choice on the path of life I would follow. I had many singing jobs and opportunities offered to me in Los Angeles. I prayed for guidance and chose not the road to "stardom," but rather the path of service to mankind. Master, no doubt, guided this decision, and it is one I have never regretted.

Master did not speak to me directly very often. I was almost always with my mother and others that surrounded him following services. When he spoke to all of us, I paid full attention and followed his direction. It is hard to recall times he chose to speak only to me. I believe that most of his personal messages came to me in writing through his letters of guidance.

Master had a behavior characteristic that I noticed he used quite often. He would preface remarks that were intended to teach a point by asking, "Do you know?" as his forefinger was extended to eye level. This emphasized what he wanted the student to learn. His voice would rise at the end of the inquiry. One day during greeting time, he raised the *teaching finger* and asked me if I knew I needed to lose flesh. That's all he said. He was well aware that, in those days, no one overweight could obtain jobs singing in public. I needed to earn money for my education so that was probably why I received that admonition, as well as for health reasons. I weighed almost one hundred and ninety pounds before he told me. It took a year of perseverance and Master's help before sixty pounds took flight forever.

Remembrances of meditating with Master are recalled vividly. When I was about twelve years old, my mother and I attended an all day Christmas meditation at Headquarters. Master led the service and the flower-bedecked room was filled to overflowing with devotees. I asked my mother what to expect, as an all day anything seems never-ending when you are twelve. She told me we were going to join in the services and sing and meditate. I wondered how in the world I could sit still for that long!

The answer to sitting still so long turned out to be *not in this world*, but rather in a heavenly meeting of peace, love, and joy. As Master began the service, the room became very quiet. His voice was sweet and loving as he explained the true meaning of Christmas. The time just flew by and I was amazed that I'd made it through the entire day without fidgeting or nodding one time. The Kriya initiation was also given, with Master guiding us through the ceremony, and I was blessed at that young age to become one of the Kriyabans. I remember, so vividly, his questioning voice asking if we accepted him as our Guru. We were then required to accept him verbally and spiritually from that time forward. God's power and love were strong in the room; the long hours we spent there placed a peaceful center in my heart and calmed any wish to leave early.

A note of interest about the Kriya ceremony. A donation of fruit from each person was placed on a table before the ceremony—much as the process in today's Kriya ceremony. Instead of asking the participants to pick up one of the blessed fruits upon leaving, the fruits were gathered by the monastics and nuns and taken to be made into juice. The juice was then distributed to all the Kriyabans in small paper cups for immediate consumption. In this manner, all could share equally the blessing obtained from the living fruit.

Master's center visitations were very demanding. He divided his time among three centers: Los Angeles, Encinitas, and San Diego. He often went to the desert. There, he was able to write and seek a rest from the many calls and activities that became a necessary part of his organizational work. When he did come to services, he would share some of the subjects about which he was writing. He would often say that the words given him were directly from God. He also shared descriptions of spiritual experiences. We were blessed to be amongst the first to hear the words that became *Autobiography of a Yogi*. Master correctly predicted that his book would become a best seller throughout the world.

My mother faithfully attended Paramahansaji's lectures and classes. When I was unable to attend with her, she relayed all she could about Master's philosophy. He spoke about a person's attitude toward material possessions. He instructed his listeners not to envy or covet another's possessions, but rather to give freely; and if someone admired something you possessed—give it to them. This was a hard lesson to learn coming from a limited income family, and also being a teenager. However, in time, I did learn not to cling to material things, but rather to make God my deep desire.

Regarding the subject of possessions and envy, Master made reference to wishes some people possess to pursue expensive hobbies, or live in affluent homes, or stay in costly hotels amidst beautiful surroundings with an attentive staff. He said while you were in a lovely place don't envy those who can obtain these surroundings as they desire. So that you are not envious, he taught, just pretend that you own all the surroundings and employ the staff. That way you can enjoy the benefits without having to pay the bills, or have the problems that come with maintenance and supervision. A lesson to all in stress-free living!

A vivid example of Master's humor keeps entering my mind. He laughed heartily as he told of many devotees asking him who they were in previous incarnations. He especially spoke of two ladies, both of whom thought they were the same queen reincarnated! He explained that it should, absolutely, make no difference who we were in the other lives, but that we should be expending our energies now—in this life—to become the best child of God that we can become. So many make a fetish of, "Who was I?" that it takes one away from the thought, "Who shall I become?" Master was troubled that people might be wasting their lives trying to satisfy their egos. He said who you were should have no bearing on your present life. Who you are becoming is the emphasis you should make. Grow in the now and let the past take care of itself—you cannot change the past. Everything you do now should change your future spiritual level of being.

Mary Peck Stockton

CHAPTER TWO

Protection

Master taught us a way to handle emergencies. I will always remember the demonstration he gave us to "disarm" our assailants. He advised us to speak in low tones with a calm demeanor and make no quick movement until the attacker was calmed by your attitude and voice. Then, when the attacker least expected it, shout loudly and make your move to flee the situation. The startle effect would disarm your enemy long enough for you to make a run for safety or help. I have applied that method a few times and found it very helpful.

I must share with you that my childhood was filled with incidents of fear and violence. When my father was serving in the navy and was away from home on sea duty, our home life was peaceful, happy, and quiet. During those times, my mother, brother, and I engaged in many learning experiences and life was full. But, when my father returned home between duties, our life became filled with chaos, violence, and fear.

Suffering from alcoholism, dysfunctional parental upbringing, poor understanding, prejudice, and hate, my father sought to make our lives miserable. As he drank he became violent, and threatened to kill us all as he chased us with his service revolver.

Many nights we hid in a cedar closet in a downstairs bedroom shaking with the fear that we'd be discovered and killed. The odor of cedar became loathsome to me as it brought back memories of our nights of terror. When we didn't take refuge in the closet, we would walk miles away from the house until morning, when my brother and I had to ready ourselves for school. We prayed together and our help was forthcoming, as my father would be asleep upon our return, or he'd left the house. At those times I was so very fearful my body shook uncontrollably, as I lived through those frightening scenes. We had no money for refuge, no transportation, or outside help. We did have God and Master's protective prayers, so that gave us courage to go on.

When my father was home, we spent much of our time in silence tiptoeing around the house so as not to disturb him or cause an outburst of temper. Sometimes days, weeks, and months were spent in silence because we feared saying or doing something that would set his temper aflame. When we saw Master he would advise my mother what our actions should be during these times, and we obeyed and remained unharmed. What a blessed contrast it was to be in Master's presence and in his vibrations and see his countenance of peace.

One terror-filled day, my father gathered us into his car (it was always identified as *his* car) to take us for a drive near the ocean cliffs. Something my mother, brother, or I said triggered my father's anger, and he drove the car straight to the edge of the precipice while repeatedly screaming, "I'm going to drive us off the edge and kill us all." Through her training by Master, my mother remained calm and we prayed silently. We dared not pray out loud as that would infuriate my father even more. In time, he became more relaxed and we continued on with the trip. Master's teachings and protection saved us, as they had so many times.

Our growing prayerful attitude and my mother's insistence to teach us prayers infuriated my father. He did all he could to discourage our religious leanings. He declared that he was an atheist. I clearly remember one Christmas Day that became the antithesis to my childhood friends' celebration of the Holy Day. We had just put up our Christmas tree and were trying to get into a happy mood. My father came downstairs, became angry, reached for the large family Bible, and systematically tore out its pages and threw them into the burning fire.

In retrospect, I am able to forgive him. God has given me the understanding to realize what a painful childhood he had. His own childhood abuse was the basis of his violent actions toward us. He did not have the spiritual guidance and knowledge that we had. He must have been tortured by the scene of Christmas joy we were trying to create.

These early experiences prepared me for many new tests. Yes, I have forgiven—but not forgotten. They became lessons for me to better my life, and help all those around me to understand people's actions.

While visiting in Encinitas with Brother Mitrananda in 1998, I shared some of my childhood experiences. He told me that, because I had learned to live through them and became aware of Master's guidance and protection, I was better prepared to face future adversities with courage. I truly believe this. It is certain that tests will be brought back to us over and over until we do learn.

My brother graduated from college during World War II and became a navy pilot. He flew a dive-bomber under the command of Admiral Chester Nimitz in the Pacific theatre of war. His assigned duty was to bomb enemy ships. At the time of his service, the battles were frequent and extreme, and he stayed in the Pacific for four years straight without a break. He was aboard the aircraft carrier Lexington when it was hit by Japanese kamikaze airplanes. These were Japanese suicide missions. The pilots used their planes as bombs, diving and exploding them into ships, and dying in the attempt. When the Lexington was hit, many of his best friends were killed. My brother often returned from his missions to the aircraft carrier with numerous machine gun holes in his plane, but not once was his body hurt! He always said that he took God with him on those flights, and you can be sure that Master was there with him.

From Master's training, my brother found it difficult to be the cause of anyone's death. Still, he flew his missions to fulfill his duty. Master taught us to fulfill our God-given duties no matter where we are. On a particular mission, he sank one of Japan's largest aircraft carriers. Its destruction changed the course of the war in the Pacific, saving many lives. He received the Navy Cross for his part in this action. After four years of intense combat action, he was allowed to come home without suffering one scratch throughout the war. Master's prayers—and ours—were answered.

During World War II, college girls were invited to attend dances at neighboring naval stations, marine bases, and army posts to help raise the morale of servicemen. All arrangements were made by the United Service Organization (USO), and we were transported by bus to various locations with security afforded us at all times. I attended quite a number of these parties and also used my singing talent to entertain very large audiences of young soldiers, sailors, and marines. At times, there were more than ten thousand in the audience. I felt quite secure as I went from place to place unharmed, and I certainly felt I was contributing to the war effort.

One party I attended was held in a building near Balboa Park in San Diego. Actually, we were not very far from the San Diego SRF Center. Some girls were asked by a group of the men to "stroll" with them in the park. We felt it would be all right and we obtained permission to leave from those in charge of the dance. Once out in the park our paths went different ways, and one officer guided me in a direction opposite from the others. Trusting as I was, I went along, not knowing his personal plans. Suddenly, I was thrown to the ground, dragged under a low-branched tree, and was attacked. I remembered Master's instructions and stayed calm. Most assuredly, Master's protection was guiding me. I was released unharmed and allowed to get up and pursue my path back to the safety of the others. The training that I received from Master and my will saw me through another hard test of living in this world.

When I attended graduate school at the University of Southern California, I had barely enough money to pay my tuition. My mother helped me by selling some of my father's bonds at a great bodily risk to herself. Nine hundred dollars was all that I had to pay for tuition, rent, and food for a year. I did manage to get a small stipend as a student assistant. I reported for my work at the speech-hearing clinic at 7:00 a.m. and then went on to classes. When my classes were over for the day, I would ready myself to sing with a small band and get any solo work that would pay. My earnings were few, but my determination to graduate was huge—I knew that education was the only way I could obtain my goals. I was often very hungry and tired, but however difficult the struggle, I felt it was imperative to complete my master's degree as soon as I could. While attending graduate school, I was confronted with decisions that required all the prayer and guidance I had learned from the "polestar" of my life. The teachings of my Guru led me to choose the right path in each instance.

CHAPTER THREE

Guidance

During my graduate school days, I sometimes would become discouraged and fatigued. At those times, I felt a great "drawing" to attend the Hollywood Church. The "call" from Master was so strong that I would forego my need for rest and food. Often, I would take my last quarter and deposit it in the streetcar coin box. That would begin my journey to meet a connecting bus line that eventually delivered me to church.

When I arrived at the church I slipped into the back row—from there I could get a good view of Master sitting on the elevated stage. I also observed Daya Mata (then Faye Wright) taking notes of all Master said. As I participated in the service, I felt a great comfort—peace encompassed me and strengthened my resolve to go on. When the collection basket was passed, I had not much to give, but gave willingly as best I could. At the end of the service, people hurried to meet with Master; I was unable to stay because I needed to catch the streetcar and return to school and my studies. Years later, Sri Daya Mata informed me that both Master and she were aware of my presence at the services.

As a student employee of U.S.C., I was asked to welcome and act as a tour guide for influential visitors. One such assignment was to greet the president of the University of Chung-king who was a distinguished campus visitor that day. He was most gracious and he seemed to approve of my skills as a hostess as well as my educational pursuits. We compared similarities and differences between U.S.C. and the University of Chung-king, China. I felt a sense of pride while talking about my school. The University of Southern California was one of the leading universities anywhere at that time. (Is my school loyalty showing?)

When our time of visitation came to an end, the president asked me to consider coming to China to be his assistant at the University of Chung-king. I took his offer under advisement and spoke to my professors and fellow students. When I came to Master in prayer, a strong intuitive response said, "No, no, you must not go." I declined the flattering offer, wondering if I'd ever get such a great chance again.

It was not too long after the president had returned to Chung-king when the news report came that Communist soldiers had overthrown the government and, in carrying out the "cleansing," had murdered the president and some faculty and staff at the University of Chung-king! God and Guru had intervened and I was no doubt saved from an abrupt departure from this earth.

I was a very young college student because I had been allowed to take college classes while still attending high school. I was quite an innocent and unworldly person, so my teachers and older student friends tended to look after my well being. They were on-the-spot "angels" who occasionally saw to it I had food and small paying campus jobs. Acting as a tour guide on another occasion, I was, once again, protected in an unfavorable situation. On this day, a very wealthy visitor came to tour the campus. He was a prospective donor to the university so I felt honor-bound to give him an A-number-one tour and an explanation of educational advantages at U.S.C.

As we strolled through the campus, he expressed an interest in my personal financial circumstances. This interest I took to mean was for the purpose of understanding some of the problems of the students. I told him I was working my way through the university by singing nights and working as a student assistant. He asked me about my living arrangements and I told him that I slept on a cot in a friend's room in the girls' dormitory for fifteen dollars a month.

The wealthy visitor seemed to react to my honest efforts to achieve my education. He asked, "How would you like your own apartment, paid tuition, and a nice monthly allowance?" I couldn't believe what I was hearing! I studied his face and intuitively received the answer, and I asked him in an innocent manner, "Do you mean free?" At my response, the wealthy person's face changed demeanor. He flushed red as he turned on his heel and said, "Oh, never mind." The tour was over. Master had protected me once again with his intuitive guidance. Materialism had not won over truth, innocence, and sincerity.

Sincerity and understanding were two of the major personality traits Master urged us to develop. He taught us to pray for understanding so that no matter what trials and tests may befall us, we would learn their purpose for our spiritual growth.

I corresponded with Paramahansaji and Daya Mata for years. I have kept and cherished their letters to this day. Sadly, some of Master's letters were lost in a flood. Sri Daya Mata and I still correspond. Her letters offer me compassion and are filled with an overpowering love that always touches my heart. Whenever I requested supportive prayers, she and SRF have always been there offering me hope, guidance, and love. Truly, SRF has shaped and guided me throughout my entire life.

I returned to San Diego upon my graduation from U.S.C. My first position was as a speech and hearing consultant serving on the staff of the San Diego County Superintendent of Schools. My service territory was the entire San Diego County. I knew the county well because my mother had taken us on short excursions throughout the area when we were children. These "investigative trips" helped prepare me for the many long miles I drove. The territory took me to mountains, deserts, and seaside towns, including Encinitas. My goal was to test every child in the San Diego school system, and provide the children with a therapeutic plan to help those with speech and hearing difficulties.

I held meetings with teachers and parents and sought

medical help for those children in need; I also raised funds to buy hearing aids and equipment, as well as maintaining a teaching schedule to help the children. Some of the last one room schools in America were in the back country of San Diego, and many times I would make home calls to the poor, to find living conditions for children very harsh. I considered myself fortunate to have had the upbringing I was given.

After a year in that school position, I married a fellow student at U.S.C. and moved to Spokane, Washington. I accepted employment as speech and hearing consultant on the Spokane city schools superintendent's staff, which served all schools from kindergarten through high school. While I was employed in Spokane, a representative from the University of Idaho offered me a summer position teaching speech pathology and audiology on their campus. I accepted and moved, for the summer, into an apartment loaned me by a faculty member.

During my stay in Moscow, Idaho, one of my students contracted bulbar polio and died. I became quite ill, and it was assumed I had contracted bulbar polio, also. I returned to Spokane and recovered from the illness. Again, it wasn't my time to go—many prayers upheld me, once more.

During a visit to my mother in San Diego in 1950, she told me that Paramahansaji wanted to see me. As my husband and I were returning to Spokane, we routed our trip through Los Angeles so that I could stop at Mother Center. This visit would become the last time I saw Master in the body.

I was directed to Master's rooms on the top floor of Headquarters; I noticed mementos from his trip to India displayed throughout the room, where he was sitting in his favorite overstuffed chair. A long woven scarf, often draped over his shoulders, was placed on the back of his chair. His face was very serene, and a slight smile crossed his lips as I stood before his quiet presence.

All proper protocol of greeting was forgotten as I faced him. I was remiss in remembering that I should honor him with a pranam. This oversight would bother me for years as I recalled I had not properly greeted Master. Daya Ma, in later years, gave me the opportunity to rectify my behavior.

I felt so unworthy to be allowed to see him and I really wondered why he had wanted to see me. I told him of my continuing work. As he patiently listened, another smile came forth as he revealed news that, at that time, I did not know. He informed me that I was going to have a baby boy, and that he would always—spiritually—watch over him. He asked me to send a picture of him when he was born. I had not entered Master's room knowing I was pregnant. Needless to say, I remembered Master's words when Peter, my son, was born. I kept my promise to send a picture. Master has kept his promise to guard over and care for my son throughout his entire lifetime. How truly blessed we are.

During the entire time I lived in Spokane, Master corresponded with me. He gave me guidance and encouragement throughout a marriage that was not going well. He urged me to keep trying and his message became, "meditate, meditate, meditate!" He was my anchor throughout difficult times. When my husband and I left Spokane and returned to San Diego we purchased my mother's home. I felt all would be well. After we had lived in San Diego for a year, my husband was offered a position in Riverside, California and we moved there and built a small home. The marriage continued to deteriorate and we divorced.

In 1952, while living in Riverside, California, I had not connected with any group of SRF devotees. The divorce from my son's father placed the total responsibility of support for my mother and son on my shoulders.

When news of Master's passing reached us, I was living in such a personal hell that I could not feel or bear the grief of his death. I lost my polestar! How could I seek comfort and guidance? My mother and I discussed the circumstances of his passing. We both "took" it in stride and I didn't allow myself a grieving period. I read the newspaper account of his immutable body and I felt honored I was allowed to know him.

Somehow the news of Master's passing was not a total shock to me. When I last spoke to him face-to-face at Mount Washington, the thought crossed my mind that I might not see him again. His body was thinner, his vitality was more withdrawn, and his hair was no longer full. The illnesses I assumed he had taken on for others seemed to have left their marks on his body. I silently pondered how much longer he would be alive.

When I read of his passing, I wondered if he had read my thoughts. I questioned whether those thoughts were given to prepare me for his departure. I did not allow myself to grieve, for it was taught in my family that one does not grieve. However, when I read in the memorial booklet of his passing, my heart became heavy. As I re-read the booklet in the ensuing years, I allowed myself to realize his departure. I looked on the picture of his face in death that held the same sweet expression I had been able to view while he was alive.

I empathized with Daya Mata and felt her pain of loss. I fully understood her description of the comforting "feeling" that encompassed her. I know that blessed feeling and I know it is Master's spirit. I believe that during the time of SRF's great loss, I could not have held up under or taken any more of the heavy burden I was already carrying. In retrospect, it's almost as though I was in denial to protect myself from deeply grieving—as though Master had prepared me to carry on in any eventuality that presented itself to me—I had been taught to never give in nor give up. As I now allow myself to realize the loss of his bodily presence on earth, I am able to realize his spirit is upholding me—my grief now takes the form of sweet remembrance.

Today when I pick up the memorial booklet, I find that I am able to let myself truly grieve in my heart—and I am able to cry. Master, in his sweet way, has led me slowly into the grieving process and, all along, has spiritually been by my side. He never left me, he never has, and I know from all my experiences that he never will.

I recall at the time of Master's passing, I felt the loss, but I was never fearful. I strongly believed we would always find care when we needed it.

Because I had no SRF church connection at the time of Master's passing, I did not have the comfort from a group that could help me. Times became harder for me. I attended churches of all kinds. The social support I received was not what I needed. I tried to find a foothold. Attending others' services did nothing to feed my soul.

Although for years I was "on my own" without an SRF group to guide me, I remained loyal. After Master's passing, I still wrote to Daya Ma. My mother and I kept in touch with Mother Center. Daya Ma supported us with her loving guidance throughout the years. I am still in possession of letters written over a period of sixty years from Daya Ma to my mother and me.

Following my divorce, I needed to find substantial employment, so I applied to the Riverside County Superintendent of Schools where I was hired immediately as speech pathologist and audiologist. Again, my work took me from one corner of the county to another; this time Riverside County. The territory extended to the Arizona border that took many hours to traverse. My brother had given me an old Chevrolet that had cost him ten dollars. I painted it robins egg blue and was confident that it would get me everywhere safely, and it did—it transported me across the desert for the next eight years.

In those days, there were no seat belts, and I was not blessed with air conditioning. The heat would rise to 120 degrees in the desert. Still, I had no car troubles, not even a flat tire, and always arrived safely at my destination. I knew no fear because Master assured us we were cared for no matter what befell us. This was proven to me so very many times. If a test arose, I would remember his words of comfort and cast fear aside. His words became true in every instance of my life.

A representative from the University of California, Los Angeles asked me to teach a course that would train teachers to understand and help children with speech and hearing difficulties. There was a newly formed campus of the University of California in Riverside. I was contracted to teach extension classes for UCLA there. This work was in addition to my full-time position on the staff of the Riverside Superintendent of Schools. Beyond those activities, I became a visiting lecturer at the University of Redlands in Redlands, California. That campus was not too far distant from Riverside, so I managed those lectures, in addition to my regular workdays.

Stress and fatigue were building, as I tried to be a consistent, productive worker, as well as a good mother and dutiful daughter. While I was still employed at the Riverside

County Schools office, the opportunity came for me to serve even further by taking an additional consultant job at the Sister Kenny Hospital in Covina, California. Tired as I was after my regular day was finished, I accepted the challenge. One day I completed my rounds of counseling patients at the hospital and wearily headed toward my home in Riverside. I was so happy to be able to drive my newly purchased car—my very first brand new car! I swung into traffic, and traveled toward Kellogg Hill, also known as "Death Hill." This hill was the scene of many deadly accidents and, at that time, was in the process of repair.

As I approached the top of the hill, a car came careening directly at me. I knew I was going to be hit, but I was boxed in the middle of traffic and there was no space to escape. Master's training came to me again, reminding me to stay calm. As I gripped the steering wheel, I kept my fingers on the ignition key. I planned to turn off the engine before I was hit to avoid fire. I was not afraid—I was surrounded by peace as I watched the car rapidly approaching our head-on collision. Before the impact, I felt that I was in a dream. I called for God's protection.

After the crash, when I woke up, I found not only had I been hit head-on, but also the car in back of me and the one on my right side had been part of the collision. I was now on the floorboards of the front seat area—virtually all that was left of my brand new, two-weeks-old car. The impact from my head had dented both side posts of the windshield. My foot was broken and jammed into the side of the steering post. Also, my chest was slightly crushed by the steering wheel that I had been holding tightly when I was thrust forward. The crash totaled the car, but I was alive and would recover, to return to limited work.

At the time of the accident my mother was taking care of my six-year-old son in Riverside, and I needed to contact her about what had happened. Also, I realized I must find a ride home, some twenty miles away. Someone stopped to ask how they might help me so I asked the "visiting angel" to inform my family of the accident. After I gave her my mother's phone number, I was taken by ambulance to the hospital, along with two of the children who were in the car that hit me. The children were very upset and shaken and I comforted them as best I could. I then lost consciousness and didn't come to again until I was in the hospital emergency room.

When I regained consciousness, I saw bloody bodies all around the emergency room; many were from different accidents that had occurred about the same time as mine. Four teenagers, who had not been involved in my accident, had died. The male who drove the car that hit me and his wife were also in the emergency room; he had been drinking. The top of his skull was partially cut off and the attendants were replacing his brain matter. His wife's back was split open and her spine was visible. I thanked God and Guru that I had emerged from such a terrible accident with only the injuries I had incurred. Even though my car was totaled—I wasn't. Again, I was thankful for my protection.

As a result of weakness from the head-on collision, I found it increasingly difficult to drive the long hours it took to serve all of Riverside County. My spine began to shoot terrible pains into my back and legs. One day, while driving back to my office, I was totally unable to move my legs. I pulled the car to the side of the road and turned off the key. I sat there for a long time and waited for some feeling to return. When I felt I could do so, I started the car and drove directly to the hospital emergency room. An orthopedic surgeon was called in and he hospitalized me immediately.

I lay in the hospital in traction for one month. After a series of tests, I was told that surgery was necessary. I underwent the severe surgery that would stabilize and make immobile the entire lower portion of my spine, and I was required to wear a steel brace from my neck to my knees for a year. I was in and out of bed for most of that time and I was told I might never be able to walk or carry out my duties. Everyone's prayers and Master's help proved that pronouncement to be untrue. After a year's time, I recovered and was able to assume my duties once again. There is nothing impossible with God!

Because of all the trials I had to face with no one but my mother to help, I felt it might be wise to be married. I was hopeful that, perhaps, another try at marriage might provide security for my son and me. Peter, my son, was nine years old and I felt he needed a male influence to help guide him.

I was "swept off my feet" by a dashing, well-to-do man who seemed to be stable and kind. Most of all I was impressed with his love for my son and his willingness to help raise him. After being married for a few years, we were blessed with our lovely daughter, Mary Caroline. She was a delight to us and brought us many happy days shared in family outings.

At that time my husband was president of an electronics firm that contributed to the U.S. space program.

I busied myself with motherhood and sang in the Los Angeles Oratorio Society. I became president of the Community Coordinating Council in Granada Hills, a suburb of Los Angeles. In that position I led the community in raising funds to place a children's library in the existing library system. Mayor Sam Yorty and Chancellor Rufus B. Von Kleinschmidt of the University of Southern California were present on the dedication day, and were quite pleased with our accomplishment.

I was certainly enjoying life as I had daydreamed it should be in the time of my youth — I was married to a man of influence and money. I was free to pursue my music and serve in civic duties. I had two wonderful children; both of them were physically perfect and above average mentally. I was happy in my little plastic world ... I thought. As I drove down the main street of our town in my brand new Cadillac,

I thanked God for all His goodness to me. I was thinking it was a very nice materialistic world in which I was placed.

It wasn't two weeks after that sublime dream that I was handed a rude awakening—an awakening for which I am now grateful. It caused me enough upheaval to, once again, plant my feet firmly on the spiritual path. I learned that no matter what happens to us, with God's and Guru's help you can survive and even do better. I learned—oh so well—that material things, per se, do not a happy life make.

Apparently, at that time, my husband had developed plans for his personal life that did not include his small family. At Christmas time he announced that he wanted a divorce so that he could marry his secretary. He left us when Mary was two years old and Peter was thirteen. He left us with no money, a house to sell that I had originally purchased, and with nowhere to go. He had not wanted me to work during our marriage, so I had not been employed for five years. I was not too confident about taking up the reins again.

I had seventeen dollars in my pocket for our support so I immediately took a job in the field of executive placement on Wilshire Boulevard in Los Angeles. The job went well, but it was paid only by commission. It was not enough security to support my growing family.

I had to sell the house at a drastic loss and move immediately to seek employment elsewhere. My mother was kind enough to offer us shelter and help in her home, so we moved back to Riverside. I obtained a position as school psychologist in Chino, California. My mother co-signed a loan so that I could obtain a small home for my children and me. The home was in Riverside.

Working in Chino meant driving quite a distance during the very early hours in the morning, as well as driving home in the dark after work. I was forced to leave Mary with a baby sitter at 5:00 a.m., which was a torturous schedule for our family. That arrangement placed us under a great deal of stress.

I was fortunate to receive a phone call from a school district in Redlands that was closer to my home in Riverside. They offered me a wonderful position on the superintendent's staff. In that administrative position, I was able to head a federal program that provided for the children who were disadvantaged and ill. I was instrumental in developing a plan for pre-school clinics to determine physical, mental, and emotional problems. My staff was able to address these problems at the beginning of a child's school experience. We provided counseling, shelter, food, clothing, proper placement, and general stability for these children. I was very happy to be serving God and Master in such a wonderful setting.

An opportunity for employment at Seattle University, a private institution in the state of Washington with an excellent educational reputation, was offered to me in 1968. I had always been interested in higher education so I saw this as a wonderful challenge. The position I was offered was Director of First Humanities, an administrative position to help guide students into their chosen majors. Also, at this time, my son was graduating from high school and I was concerned about his future education. I had very little money and with this job my son would be offered a four-year scholarship to attend the university. Here was an opportunity to expand my knowledge and service, and also provide for my son's college education. I accepted the offer and moved my son and daughter and all our possessions to Bellevue, Washington, a city just a few miles from Seattle.

When I moved from Riverside to Seattle, I was embraced by the Catholic traditions. Since my work was at a Catholic university, I attended Mass there. I never withdrew my heart from SRF. I certainly instituted the SRF teachings in the counseling and guidance that I gave to students, but I didn't have a meditation group to support me.

Along with my new position guiding students to their course work and future job opportunities, my work also included assisting the academic vice-president. He assigned me the task of organizing and directing student orientation. Another assignment was to prepare the logistics for the accreditation team that would evaluate Seattle University's standing in the academic world. Following the evaluation, we received the highest rating obtainable, a rating for which we were extremely grateful.

Another time, I was assigned the responsibility of organizing large community-based functions. There was quite a stir when I suggested that the faculty convocation be held in the middle of the central area of Seattle. The central area was home to many economically disadvantaged persons; it also had a large population of community activists. These were the turbulent times in the 60's with anti-war demonstrations taking place and, at times, there were actual acts of civil disobedience. Our campus was invaded by protestors in one instance that led to violence. I felt it would be a positive move for the faculty to meet with people of the surrounding area in their space and use their buildings for our meetings. TV reporters and security guards were present to document and control the activity. As an outcome, the convocation became the beginning of positive community-based interaction.

Later, when the university built a beautiful new gymnasium, the young people who lived in the central area were invited to use the facilities. Many children took advantage of the offer and joined the Boys' and Girls' Club of America that met in the gymnasium. Father J. A. Fitterer, the president of the university at that time, was given a national award for his generous participation in the organization. God's unconditional love in practice!

In my first year at the university, I was also responsible for planning and supervising special social occasions. This included ordering food, instructing service people, and arranging entertainment for up to five thousand parents and friends of the university. Such diverse work was extremely interesting to me, but also very stressful. The intensity of the work took its toll on my health and, in the middle of the accreditation process, I was stricken with an illness that would require surgery. I told the doctor he'd have to wait until I had completed my tasks. He smiled and said, "You'll be back soon," and I was. That particular surgery took a month for my recovery, but at least I had completed my university assignment!

Hard times fell on Seattle financially in 1970. In fact, there was a famous billboard that said: "The last one to leave Seattle—turn out the lights." The depression affected the total community, including the university, and a re-evaluation of its financial status was necessary. In addition, anti-war demonstrations were becoming more prevalent. Many students blocked admittance to the campus of Seattle University, and to the Seattle Community College campus as well. In the midst of these upsetting times came major unemployment throughout the area. I felt I should go elsewhere for our safety and peace. I reorganized the duties of my position and resigned with a letter to the administration that would help them save money on the position I had filled.

Never before had I needed to search for employment. Generally, I had job offers while I was employed elsewhere, so I was confident that I could obtain immediate employment somewhere out of the troubled area of Seattle. How wrong I was! After sending many job applications, and after developing deep concern for our welfare, I was forced to re-member the motto on which I was raised: "There's nothing impossible with God!" I clung to my faith and prayers and, at last, found a position heading the women's programs at Everett Community College, a highly rated two-year college about thirty miles north of Seattle.

I sold my house in Bellevue and found temporary living quarters in Forest Park (a smaller city north of Seattle), while I fulfilled my contract with the university. As my daughter, now eight years old, and I were traveling to our temporary home, we approached a signal light in Forest Park. I looked in my rear view mirror and saw another car approaching at high speed—it was evident that the driver was out of control and was not going to stop. We were positioned with cars in front of us so there was no place to turn away from a sure rear-end collision. I told my daughter to hold on and placed my right arm over her chest to ease the blows we were both about to receive; with my left arm I held firmly onto the steer-ing wheel. My thought was, "God help us!" We were hit full force by an automobile driven by a drug addict on his way to receive methadone treatment.

The accident occurred directly in front of the city hall police station. The police chief came out of the building, arrested the man on the spot, and told me that he would vouch for my innocence in the matter of any accident fault. I was stunned by the impact; my car was totaled and, for awhile, I couldn't remember our temporary rental house address. We had no family close by, and we were on our own. Just at the moment I needed someone, a lovely young lady came up to me and offered assistance. She told me that she was a graduate student at the University of Washington and that she'd stay with us to help us through our difficulty. Master had sent an angel!

This angel cared for us through our recovery period. When we were capable of taking care of ourselves, she left us after a loving goodbye. Once again a demonstration of God's care through our trials.

When we moved to Everett, Washington, I knew no one. We obtained an apartment near my new work at Everett Community College. As I began to meet people, I volunteered for community service. I had been single now for ten years. I kept feeling that I should open my mind to consider re-marriage for my daughter's sake. I'd met a variety of people from my contact in previous community service, and I had decided that it was best to stay alone if I could not find a spiritually minded husband. He must, I felt, realize my need for prayer and meditation. God came first in my life, and anyone I chose must understand that.

Part of my community service work was to serve on the board of directors of the local March of Dimes chapter. At the meetings I met a widower, David Stockton, a fine person who also served on the board. I had managed to buy a small house situated on a high bluff overlooking the bay in Everett, and he lived only a few blocks from us. My daughter took it upon herself to invite Mr. Stockton to dinner. She told him that I had issued the invitation. She then came home to announce her plan. Our cupid repeatedly set up situations that brought us together.

One evening Mr. Stockton and I were sitting on the back steps of my house watching the sunset over the water. The subject of religion came up and I told him of my lifelong acquaintance with Paramahansaji and SRF. To my amazement, he had read *Autobiography of a Yogi* and had sent for the lessons!

A few days later, I was driving to town through our neighborhood and passed Mr. Stockton's house. I saw him slowly walking down the street. A very strong impression (intuitive voice) said to me, "There is your husband." We know it was Master who brought us together.

After David and I married, we began to attend SRF services at the center on Stone Way in Seattle, Washington. It was quite a long way to drive to church, but we enjoyed being with "Master's children." My health began to wane from overwork and stress. One Christmas I announced to David that I'd like to attend the all-day Christmas meditation. It had been a "given" that we would be with all his family in Tacoma, so my request didn't sit well. How could he explain my absence from the family gathering? Regardless, I attended the meditation while David drove on to his appearance in Tacoma. I suppose I was misunderstood, but I knew I must attend that meditation. It brought me better health and happiness and I shall always be glad that I attended.

After we attended church services at Stone Way in Seattle for awhile, the group then moved farther north in Seattle to 65th Street, where we attended regularly. Our home was then in Bellevue, Washington, so the trip to church was more convenient. We were delighted when the present church site on Serpentine Way in the Shoreline District of Seattle was purchased. There we wholeheartedly joined into the group. We shared the pictures of the building's reconstruction and makeover with Daya Mata in 1996.

David and I continue to study lessons together and live as closely as we can to the ideals of SRF. We read and discuss the weekly "lectures" that I had been so very privileged to hear directly from Master. His guidance is still here! His words come alive to me as I can still recall and almost hear his voice saying them.

As I was writing the previous information, the following message was intuitively received. I write it in service to Master to pass it on to you. He wanted us to know that even though we haven't seen, heard, or directly "felt" his presence in person, he is here, near, and always responsive to the true heart that seeks him. He tells us that his spirit will never die, for he lives to comfort, guide, and love us. He urges us to seek him in the silent times of our day—talk to him, ask him. Even though we don't see the lights, hear sounds, etc., *we will receive an answer.* He said to wait patiently and be open to receive his silent love and guiding principles of life.

God comes through to us in Master's teaching and counsel. Even if you can't attend an SRF group—pray, read, meditate. Join the Worldwide Prayer Circle in spirit. Lend the strength of your spirit to ask for peace and blessings. You will receive results, as I have, through the peaceful silence of your soul. Never lose heart. God doesn't give up on us. Don't give up praying, and communing with Him. Speak to your Guru with your total love and he will carry that love to God.

During our first year of marriage, we had a particularly hard rainy season. The roof began to leak and it was necessary for us to collect rainwater in containers placed throughout the living room and bedrooms. Our budget couldn't accommodate the large purchase of a new roof. We prayed about it and I suggested that we take a walk to relieve the stress of worry.

As we walked along, I had a strong impression to buy some scratch lottery tickets. We came to a large grocery store and David purchased a couple of tickets. His eyes widened as he scratched one of the tickets and uncovered its numbers. He said, "I think we won!" I looked at the ticket and told him it was his desire to win that had clouded his vision. It was close, but not a winner.

I was still following my intuition as we proceeded on our walk. After a couple of blocks we saw a convenience store across the street. I said, "David, please go buy three tickets at that store and the winner will be the third ticket."

As we were entering the store, a lady forced her way in

front of David and took her place in front of him at the ticket counter. He was a bit miffed, but stepped back and allowed her to proceed without comment. He watched in silence as she bought ten tickets. David then bought three tickets, as I had asked. We retreated to a quiet part of the store and scratched the first ticket, then the second, to no avail. The third ticket scratched hit pay dirt and he whispered, "I think we've won." Three figures matched—we had won ten thousand dollars! Had the rude lady not forced her way in front of David, the winning ticket would have been one of the ten she had purchased; instead, we now had the money for a new roof! Blessed help received!

A week later, David followed his intuition and bought one lottery ticket that yielded a prize of one thousand dollars! Our needs were met and we received more than we actually needed at that time for a new roof. Quoting from Malachi:

"Prove me now herewith saith the Lord of hosts, if I will not open you the windows of heaven, and pour you out a blessing, that there shall not be room enough to receive it."

As we had prayed for assistance, blessings were given us abundantly.

Mary Peck Stockton

CHAPTER FOUR

A Trip to Heaven with Master

Mary Peck Stockton

In November 1983, I was told that I had colon cancer. Somehow, the news did not frighten me. After I left the doctor's office, I called Mother Center to ask for supportive prayers. Surgery to remove the cancer was performed as soon as possible. Because of an inherited blood disease and the surgical procedures, my prognosis for recovery was not good. I had lost almost all my blood, which needed to be replaced over the days following the surgery.

I was told that I might not live many more days. Upon hearing the news, I lay back in my hospital bed and surrendered completely to God, telling Him that I was ready and willing to come home. I want to have you understand that, at that time, the drugs from the surgery had worn off, and I was fully awake.

When I relaxed, fixed my gaze on the spiritual eye and totally let go, I began to have a life-changing experience. Though at death's door, I felt truly alive and my spirit soared. I began to hear music fill the room. I looked around to be sure there was no radio playing, nor was the television on. I had a single room because of my serious condition, so I knew the music could only be coming from heavenly sources.

Suddenly, I saw terrible writings all over the walls of the

room. Frightening moments of sound and vision were displayed before me. It was a vile and loathsome vision that forced me to call from within the very depths of my soul to reach for courage. I declared in a loud voice, "I belong to God Almighty." Instantly, the upsetting vision disappeared. (Later I was told by Daya Ma that the frightening experience I had was representing to me things I must change in myself.)

After the evil vision disappeared and I repeated my allegiance to God, I began to hear vocal music surrounding me. Unseen angels were singing instructions to me, assuring me. I asked the nurse, who had walked into the room, if she saw or heard anything, and she told me that she didn't. She said that I should relax, and then she asked me if I was afraid to die. I told her I didn't think I was.

When the nurse left the room and I lay back on my bed, I felt a warm, soft hand take my right hand, and I was told intuitively not to be afraid. It was Master!

I looked at the foot of my bed and was startled to see my mother's full body materialize in front of me. She was praying for me and asking God to take her instead of me. I felt her tweak my toe as she often did affectionately when I was ill. At that time my mother was actually living in California. She was unable to travel to the hospital to be with me, but through God's grace, she was able to make an appearance in spirit.

I then began to see visions of numerous people in front of

me. I saw Paramahansaji smiling and reassuring me. The group of people with him beckoned to me to travel with them. They asked if I'd like to go with them. One of the visions identified herself as my mother's prayer partner. Another young spirit answered me in the affirmative when I asked if she was Ann, a friend who had recently died. The figure smiled and said, "I can be anyone you want me to be." After reliving some of those moments, I realize it was Babaji who had come with Master to guide me on!

I asked the group of spiritual visitors, "Am I dead?" They assured me I wasn't, but repeated their invitation for me to accompany them on a "trip." Master then asked me to go with him. Extreme peace and joy surrounded me, and I was filled with a massive amount of energy. I was so *very* happy!

Questions I had carried in my mind for years were answered instantaneously. I was conscious of the hospital room, visitors, and surrounding furnishings; yet, I was totally in another world. I felt as though I was riding on God's shoulder, and could see in two worlds at one time.

As I held tightly onto Master's hand, we traveled a long way through dark, dark space until I saw a great white wing consisting of large individual feathers. It looked to be about twelve to fifteen feet long and five feet wide. I felt invisible hands lifting me onto the wing. I knew intuitively that my father's hands were helping me to be lifted onto the wing, and I quietly thanked him. The angels' strong hands held me on the wing, and I was assured I would not fall. All the while, the angels' instructing singing voices surrounded me, and I continued to hold firmly to Master's hand.

At one time Master smiled and, with a twinkle in his eye, changed his appearance. I said, "Master, David won't recognize you—you'd better stay the same." He laughed and said, "I like being this way most." He had changed his appearance to be the youth in the turban when he first came to America.

I was transported from place to place on the giant wing. I was aware that people were existing on different spiritual levels. Intuitively, it was made clear that one must work at that level until he can be elevated to the next spiritual level. Our duty, it was explained, is to work to reach the highest level, which is God. There were all kinds of people in various garb. They were engaged in a variety of activities, and I felt I was observing a huge movie screen. I heard voices from the past that greeted me—they were people I had known and had helped in my work on earth.

I heard people praying for me by name. Each prayer was seen as a single white feather floating up and attaching itself to the wing that spiritually supported me on my journey. The prayers were actually upholding me! I knew then that prayers are, indeed, substance. They do uphold you and your dear ones.

I was taken to observe many sights and experiences. I saw a variety of soldiers in the uniforms of their countries, representing all periods of time in history. Other people shocked me with their appearance. Some seemed closer to an animal state than others. They actually had strips of hair on their bodies similar to animals. Were these evolving souls?

My travels made me realize that life is one great continuum in space. Our problems return to us repeatedly until we turn around, face them, ask for spiritual guidance, change ourselves, and resolve them. We, then, are free to move on.

At the very bottom of the spiritual planes I observed a torturous level. People were mired in the mud and rock, and were digging their way out of the river bottom. It seemed to me, at the time, that these people were the ones who made no attempt to elevate their souls with prayer during their lifetime.

After observing level after level, we traveled up and up to higher planes. Then, I was lifted even a greater distance in space, where I was led to massive golden "heavenly" gates. As we approached the golden gates, I realized they looked similar to the Mormon Tabernacle, only they were hugely more massive and pure gold. Bright rainbows of gorgeous colors shot all over the area, and I was enthralled with their beauty. Pink, coral, white, and gold rainbows surrounded the scene.

I saw two long lines of people at the entrance to the gates, waiting their turn to advance. Everyone was silent as they approached a table where an attendant checked long lists. I was aware that Master no longer held my hand, and I was directed to the line that formed on the left. I don't know why I was in the left line and others formed a line on the right, but I asked no questions.

I moved slowly up the line and suddenly I heard the voice of my son, Peter, calling for me. He was begging me to come back. He told me I was still needed by the family, and that I must come back. I heard his voice so very clearly. He was not physically in my hospital room, nor even in the state of Washington; his prayers and pleas were traveling through space prayer from California. Then a gentle voice approached me and asked me if I wanted to go back, and I said, "I guess so. My family needs me."

During the entire experience I was aware of two worlds. I was able to be responsive in both worlds. I could foresee visions of future happenings. My daughter had flown in from California unexpectedly, but I "saw" her before she arrived and told my husband to expect her. I asked him to go to a restaurant for his dinner and told him I would send my daughter to meet him when she arrived. He humored me. It was obvious that he thought I'd lost my bearings.

Upon her arrival, my daughter took one look at my face and exclaimed, "Mom, you look as though you are four years old. Your face is glowing!" I smiled and sent her on to meet her dad. While still in that state of grace, I "observed" their meeting at the restaurant. I was still in two worlds.

A nun from the hospital visited me, looked at my glowing countenance, and instantly said, "You're in heaven, aren't you?" I told her yes and she asked me to describe what I saw. She was uplifted by the spirit surrounding me and grateful to receive my report of the visions I was seeing.

The same thing happened to a social worker from the hospital who visited me. She asked me to sing to her what the angels were singing, and I was able to share that with her. She even brought an autoharp to my bedside and, as I sang the angel messages I was hearing, she played the tunes on the autoharp. I'm sure the nurses and patients wondered what was transpiring in my hospital room.

My experiences lasted five days. I was told spiritually that I should not reveal all the details of them, but that I must bring back important messages for some specific individuals still on earth.

The most important message that I carried back for everyone was that we must *forgive those who have hurt us and ask for forgiveness from those we have hurt.* It was stated: *"To forgive is to be forgiven!"* It became obvious to me that the frightening scenes I had witnessed were speaking to me of my need to change. Since I returned to earth, I have searched my memory and recalled incidents that I needed to heal. I needed to forgive!

I contacted people by phone or letter to ask for their understanding and forgiveness. To those who had passed on, I asked forgiveness in prayer. In my heart and in prayer, I systematically forgave those who had hurt me. Because I have done these things, I am more at peace than ever before. Please take this spiritual message to heart and confront your past hurtful situations with courage and love. The importance of my blessed message received in this experience should never be forgotten.

When I was released from the hospital, I volunteered as an aide for five years following my recovery. During that period I was able to counsel many patients with the same surgeries I had. The tests and problems from which I had recovered in the past had prepared me to empathize and help guide others through their ordeals.

The year following my colon cancer surgery, my husband was stricken with the same disease. His cancer was located in almost the same place my problem had existed. Again, prayers were requested and his surgery, too, was very successful. At this writing, we both have been cancer-free for over seventeen years.

CHAPTER FIVE

Forgiveness

The major message of the heavenly visit I experienced in the hospital was that I knew I must change myself. I needed to forgive those who had hurt me in the past. I knew I needed to ask forgiveness of those I had hurt.

The commission to explain forgiveness was given me to share with others that they, too, may be cleansed. It was made an imperative to me that I inform all people who read these words of the vital importance of forgiveness to soul growth.

Giving forgiveness and asking for forgiveness are very difficult tasks. I can't tell you strongly enough how important forgiveness is. We must work through our own egos and gather the courage and understanding it takes to forgive. This is something we should all do before we die. Think about it, pray for help, and do something about it. Develop your intuition, pray deeply, and He will impress you with guidance and courage.

The Bible tells us to forgive is to be forgiven. In his ten steps to God, Lord Manu points out that non-anger to a situation or person is *not* forgiveness — it is self-control. He goes on to say that forgiveness is totally forgiving the person and the actions. Others have told us that forgiving is not forgetting. You may forgive, but you don't have to forget. Just don't harbor ill will. Send love to your enemy—love can't be destroyed.

Forgiveness is not the same as condoning. It doesn't take away a person's need to be responsible for his actions. And it takes courage to face the perpetrator and yourself in asking forgiveness. It is not an easy way; it is a process that takes much work on your part. To be fair, you must tell the person with whom you are upset just why the situation is so hurtful to you. It is not right for you to be angry and not give the other person an opportunity to rectify his behavior.

Although forgiveness takes hard work, probably the easiest way to forgive is to slip into another person's shoes. Envision the circumstances in life that caused him to hurt you. You can become kinder and more forgiving when you understand what that person has had to endure that formed the controlling or mean-spirited character that has had a negative impact on your life. If you are able to form this understanding, you may be able to find in your heart the ability to forgive him.

Many times we react to negative situations by becoming controlling, to protect ourselves from being hurt further. In order to break this pattern, we must begin to sincerely "act out" respect for our fellow men, predecessors, and our children. Positive role-playing creates an acceptance for one another. By respecting others, we strengthen our own self-respect, thereby breaking the chain of self-defeating behavior.

We begin to see the value of rising above anger-induced actions (reactions), hurt feelings (ego), or the controlling of others as an unacceptable method of interaction. No longer should we say: "You have made me angry because you don't do as I tell you to do." Instead, we should say: "I will try to respect your needs and wishes because I understand what you have suffered." We need to come to a better understanding of our needs, motivations, and reactions so that we may interact peacefully. Reverse the trend that was imposed on you. Respect yourself; respect others. Then healing may be yours.

We help people by the example of our actions and words. Before you make an important statement, ask yourself, "Will I help or enrich anyone with this statement?" If not, don't say it. Also, ask yourself if the statement is true, uplifting, helpful, or kind. If it can't meet those criteria, it probably would be best to keep it to yourself. Then you will not find yourself in need of asking for forgiveness.

Think about this: If we don't surrender ourselves truthfully and completely to God and His will for us, we deceive ourselves. When we think we are winning and make the wrong choice, we are actually losing. But when we think we are losing by making the right choice, we are actually winning. God's tests for us work that way. Surrender to His guidance and all will be well.

It comes down to having the right attitude. Look to your

trials or hurts as blessings or as opportunities for improvement — don't look at them as punishments. It is the faulty ego that drives people to wrong actions and hurtful words. Get the ego under control by introspection and meditation. *Learn to forgive yourself as you forgive others.*

Move on with your God-given intuition. Trust in it. Then, in time, you will surely see why a particular situation came about and became a blessing to you. Master told us to pray deeply for the right outcome, then let go. Don't cover the seed you planted in prayer with worry before it can sprout, flower, and bloom.

You must understand that bad things may happen to good people through karma and circumstance. Focus on God and your Guru and the outcome will be positive. Knowing that all trials and tests are for a purpose, look for the purpose; learn from it and your life will change for the better. Use your will power to forge ahead with God's supporting love power. Forgive and you will be forgiven.

A direct quote from the *Mahabharata* emphasizes the importance of forgiveness. It states:

"One should forgive, under any injury. It hath been said that the continuation of the species is due to man's being forgiven. Forgiveness is holiness; by forgiveness the universe is held together. Forgiveness is the might of the mighty; forgiveness is sacrifice; forgiveness is quiet of mind. Forgiveness and gentleness are the qualities of the Self-possessed. They represent eternal values."

CHAPTER SIX

Intuition and Fear

If we listen with our hearts humbly asking for help and go quietly to God in meditation, we will surely receive an answer. The key is in the receiving. When you are blocked from some action, wait patiently—some form of answer will come. Perhaps it will be an incident or a person who will respond to that inner need. Wait—be patient—and you will see God's scenario for you open like the petals of a flower. But the key word here is to *receive*. If you busy yourself with wandering thoughts or activities, you will block the flow of inspiration. God's plan for you will be shown quietly through your "inner impression."

When I am asked to speak publicly, I go into my "inner reserve" away from everyone. Sometimes, the only preparation I make is to ask God and Guru for help. It is always forthcoming and thoughts come to mind that often answer questions that are in the listeners' minds. I know this because they have told me so following my presentation. Open yourself up to inner guidance, and your intuitive responses will help you and others.

You can't receive intuition unless you fully open your heart and mind. If you don't turn the handle of a spigot, the water can't flow. If you don't open your mind and soul with prayer,

God can't get through. The water (God's answer) is right there waiting. All you need to do is open the channel and receive. I consider intuition to be our "C" mail, in other words, cosmic "E" mail. If you learn to use true intuition wisely you can be pre-warned and guided to changes that must occur for your benefit.

Master always emphasized the need to develop intuition, through which he may speak to you and guide your thought to the right outcome. Guidance is given as you develop your intuitive process. You may hear or read a lesson over and over and you may say to yourself, Oh, yes, I've heard this before. But until you have reached the point in your development to "receive" it and really learn by it, you will not take it into the core of your being. Master prepares you for the proper time of understanding and, one day, you will hear or read the text you've heard before, but this time it will reach your soul and it will change your life for the better.

In our lifetime, my husband and I have moved a great deal. Even before we met, I would be confronted with the necessity of moving to another place. Just as I was settled in a home and had given it my personal nesting touches, I would be faced with a problem or need that required our uprooting and moving on. I envied people who lived in the same house and neighborhood for years and years. God, in His infinite wisdom, would pick me up like a mother cat and drop His kitten in a totally new setting that called for many new adjustments. Each time I thought I'd stay put, I was uprooted again and again to face new challenges. Now, in retrospect, I realize that I had learned a great deal in each circumstance.

That learning I carried with me helped me to understand and to adjust to many future challenges. These prepared me for the trials I was to undergo. I feel that all experiences helped me to grow spiritually. I did my very best in each new circumstance and then moved on. I now see, more than ever, God's plan for using me. The variety of situations in which I've lived has taught me invaluable lessons—God's wonderful educational system!

When I went to Encinitas every week with my mother, I did not fully realize the blessings I was receiving at that time. I reasoned, Master tells us God will care for us and all should have a happy life, so I just knew I'd be cared for. As I grew older, I remembered what Master told us. We will always be assured of care and we should not let fear come into our consciousness.

While counseling individuals who were fearful, I often used this illustration about the power of fear. A little boy gets on his brand new bicycle. He is unsure of his ability to control the direction of the wheels. As he wobbles down the sidewalk, he spots a large telephone pole and fear envelops him. He repeats and repeats to himself, "I'm going to hit it, I'm going to hit it." You don't need much imagination to determine what happened. He, of course, steers his newly acquired two-wheeled prize right into that hard and unyielding telephone pole. Fear brought him straight to the foot of the dreaded object. You do the same in your life if you let fear in, but if you stop fear as it tries to enter your mind and govern your destiny, you can be the winner. Remember that Master told us that his devotees would always be cared for and that we should never let fear come into our consciousness. Having complete trust is the way you must feel. Remember, we are the soul, not the body. Connect your soul to the spirit and fear cannot enter your consciousness.

I learned a valuable, tried and true method from Master's teachings to monitor my own fears and worries. At the very first indication of a wrong thought, fear, word, or action, I say to myself: "No! Stop!" while envisioning myself in the white light of God. Fear and negativity leave me immediately when I put my mind on God and His all-protecting vibration. Fill your mind with a positive word, thought, or action so that nothing but good may enter in. When you become stressed or worried, chant inwardly the Kriya song: "Roses to the left, roses to the right, roses front and behind." While doing so, place yourself in memory in the Roses Ceremony and ask God to help you. Peace will be yours.

Our time comes to pass on to the astral world only when God so desires, but remember that God and Master are always with you. Guruji's mission in this life was to assure us all that God does know each one of us and cares for our every need. He expects us to pray (meditate) and *receive* His blessing. For a time I forgot to receive, but when I did remember, I was blessed.

Be sure you open your mind only to good thoughts. Your brain acts as a computer and stores all that comes through your eyes, ears, and touch. Make sure that what you have in your spiritual computer system is good, so that it may be recalled at a time when you will need it. When something bad or wrong is introduced to you, reject it immediately, and put God, Guru, and good thoughts into your soul. Doing that, you will always be able to call on your positive supply of spiritual help.

When fear confronts you, don't let it come in. There was a recent story of a small girl lost in the woods who was found miraculously. When asked by the people who found her why she wasn't fearful, she said, "I just stayed calm." Good thoughts sustained her. She told her rescuers that she kept thinking positive thoughts of what it would be like when they found her. She said she wouldn't let herself think about what would happen if they didn't find her. No matter what happens, face fear with strong resolve and courage. Know that you are taken care of—that you belong to God, Christ, and Guru.

Master reminds us to take care of our bodies and minds. Keep them both clean and strongly active for God. Your mind controls your body. A healthy mind creates a healthy body. Right thinking, proper diet, and exercise will make you a true instrument through which God can achieve His will.

God never lets a situation or question go unanswered. A problem or test is brought to you for an answer, or to give a direction for its solution. Until the problem has been addressed correctly, it will return to you for revision. Always pray for guidance to solve each particular problem.

When you talk to God in your secret heart, ask Him to guide your thoughts to do what you should do, and that which is best for you to achieve. Concentrate about what it is you want, then think about what you must to do prepare yourself to obtain your wish. If it is education or practice, you must find the right method to achieve your goal. Then, when you do achieve it, let God lead you to your use of it.

If you have been given talent or money, use them to serve God. Let no one else interfere with your God-given guidance. Seek your soul! Don't let your life be just doing "things" and processing "stuff!" With God's guidance, you will become a true blessing to mankind. As with everything you accomplish, you must "go at it" with sincerity, and with the desire to become a better vehicle for God's work. Fear has no place in Master's teachings.

CHAPTER SEVEN

Sri Daya Mata

I have always considered it a blessed privilege to know Sri Daya Mata. When I observed her as a young woman in Encinitas, San Diego, Hollywood, and Los Angeles, she served Master in a beautifully efficient manner. I never saw any look on her sweet countenance except one of loving compassion. Her talents were many and she worked side-by-side with Master. She was secretary, cook, organizer, administrator, social director, or hostess; she served in any position that was needed to help Master achieve his goals. All of these experiences obviously prepared her for the tasks she would be asked to perform in her present role. She has always given of herself one hundred percent for the love of God and guru.

There have been many times in my life when I called upon Master and Daya Ma for guidance and help. Each of their responding letters has become treasured to me. They always contained prayerful guidance and supportive love. Daya Ma's letters, filled with such sincerity and compassion, often brought me to tears. I have considered her my truest friend. Even though many years passed from the last time I saw her in 1950 until our visit in 1996, I felt that we were always close in spirit.

As my mother lay dying in the hospital in 1995, I called

Mother Center to ask for prayers. To my astonishment, I received a return call from Daya Ma herself. She comforted me and asked me to tell my mother that Master would be caring for her, and that Daya Ma and all at Mother Center were praying for her. I approached my mother's hospital bed and repeated Daya Ma's message to her, and a look of peace came over her face. She managed to smile and say, "I love you." These words were her last. I'm sure Christ and Master were there with her. We were able to pray with her as she lay dying, and Daya Ma's last message to her brought her great peace.

After my mother's passing, I felt a need for closure. I wrote to Daya Ma requesting an audience with her. She granted my request and set up an appointment for my daughter and me. A full account of our wonderful visit may be found in Addendum A.

Daya Ma had requested a future meeting with my husband and me, so upon my return to Seattle I shared this information with David and he was pleased. Right then and there, we began to plan when we could return to Los Angeles. Some eight months later, in September 1996, I returned with my husband to visit Daya Ma. Because I had not seen Daya Ma for years before my daughter and I had visited eight months previously, Daya Ma was surprised to see us so soon. I told her it was her request to meet my husband that brought about this quick return. David has written an account of his impressions of our visit in Addendum B. My description of the visit follows in Addendum C.

David and I were greatly honored to be allowed to see Daya Ma. Sister Namita, Daya Ma's personal secretary, took photos as David and I remained seated at Daya Ma's feet. She requested copies of these photos and we were honored to comply. As we departed, Daya Ma called to Sister Namita, telling her to respond to our request for a speaker to come to Seattle Center. Upon our return to Seattle, we learned that our request had already been fulfilled; a notice had been received by the center and a speaker was scheduled.

The Seattle devotees were very interested in hearing about our visit with Daya Ma. They wanted to know how she looked, what were the surroundings, what were our feelings and impressions, and what was said and done; they had a desire to know all they could about such a memorable and sacred visit. Many asked if we would write an account of our visit, and David and I both agreed to do this and to distribute copies to those who wished to have them.

After our wonderful visit with Daya Ma, many new challenges entered our lives. More physical "trials" appeared and were passed. Intuitively, I knew our time was approaching to move on and resume our lives in a different setting. This "gnawing" kept at my heart. That was a familiar feeling to me, as I had been "prepared" in the past in the same manner. I opened my heart and mind and asked Master to place us where we should be in our new adventure.

We were pleased to hear from our daughter that she

planned to marry and move to Portland, Oregon. She'd been apart from us for many years living in California, and now she was moving closer. A short time after she and her husband moved back to the Northwest (Portland had been his boyhood home) they requested that we move closer to them so that we could help one another.

We placed our condominium in Bellevue, Washington, on the market, sold it, and moved all our belongings to Portland. We then began our next lifetime adventure in new surroundings with SRF members at the Portland Center.

Because Master had helped prepare us, we were able to move and happily adjust to our new role as grandparents when, after a year, our daughter gave birth to our granddaughter, Hannah Claire. Before her arrival, I had prayed for a beautiful soul to be sent to us from heaven, and we were given just that. Following a difficult birth, we gave support and love to the newly formed family. They, in return, have helped us. We are a happy spiritual family.

No one could believe that, throughout all my years of knowing Master and Daya Ma, I did not have the privilege of attending any of the convocations held in Los Angeles. Various major problems as well as monetary reasons kept me from attending.

In 1998 I was determined to complete the spiritual pilgrimage to honor Master I had promised myself. I knew I must make the attempt to attend that heavenly meeting where so many from the entire world gathered to honor God and Master. Our debts were unusually heavy that year; therefore, if we were going to go, we needed to make monetary adjustments. Airplane tickets and hotel costs presented quite a challenge to our budget. I did get an idea that would help. I sold some of my jewelry. That managed the cost of the airplane.

Then, out of the blue, I received a phone call from an East Indian business man who told me he was a new Kriyaban and that he was told by Master during meditation to come see me. Friends in Seattle had told this man my plight. He called and made an appointment.

He and his small family arrived for their visit. His children were young, lively and eager to explore. My husband and the visitor's wife took the small children on a walk while Master's representative and I talked. I told him some of my early experiences and showed him Master's original signature on my mother's copy of *Autobiography of a Yogi*. We shared a few wonderful moments.

He then said to me that Master had "told" him to give me some money so we could go to the convocation. I was totally taken aback at his statement, and I gratefully declined his kind offer. He insisted until I finally accepted with deep gratitude; as he wrote the check, I did not look at it. I had no idea of the amount, but expressed my thanks. I said, "I will only take this because it is from Master."

The small family returned from the walk with my husband. We exchanged pleasantries and bid a fond farewell. I thanked both the husband and wife for their wonderful gift to us. After they left, I looked at the check and was taken by surprise. So much money! The check was in the amount of $601.00. I asked my East Indian friend in Seattle why the extra one dollar. She told me that it is felt to be unlucky in India to write even numbers; therefore, the amount of $601.00. I thanked her for her friendship expressed by informing this generous man about our financial need. Remember the amount of the gift check. As my convocation story unfolds, you will learn how Master works in our lives.

Before we left for Los Angeles to attend the convocation, my husband's back began to hurt. I told him I'd be willing to go by myself. He knew how very important this trip was to me and he assured me he was getting better. He said he'd have to go so that he could help me.

We had an uneventful flight and arrived in Los Angeles. By the time we arrived at the airport, David's back pain had become terribly intense. I was able to get him a wheel chair. We met with a wonderful friend from Seattle who deposited us at the Biltmore Hotel. David, the wheel chair, the suitcases, and I went into the hotel. I made him comfortable and went to the desk to register and arrange for a special room where his wheel chair could be accommodated. His pain got much worse.

We did make it to the Bonaventure Hotel for the showing of the film about Master. After that showing, David was in such pain that he remained in our hotel room. I was unwilling to leave him to attend any meetings. All I could do was to go down to the Biltmore lobby to reunite with friends and meet a number of people from India. These were people who wanted to meet me after having read my article in the SRF magazine.

I also met with one of Master's early disciples. We exchanged fond memories of Master as we sat in front of the shrine that honored Master's passing. Before meeting with anyone, I was drawn to that shrine. I saw others pranam as I realized that was the place Master left this world. The "pull" from that area was so strong! I was overcome with a deep loving feeling of comfort and support. Master has not left us—his spirit remains where he has been.

Several hours were spent in the Biltmore lobby visiting with various people. I kept going to our room to check on David. I realized he was becoming more anxious and was suffering very deep pain. We had to make the decision that we must go back to Seattle.

David went to the front desk to pay our bill as we prepared to leave. His face turned white as the hotel clerk handed him our bill. I thought to myself that he must be in terrible pain, or we are in terrible financial trouble. He made his way to my side. I said, "Are you all right? Did you have to put a lot on our Visa?" He smiled and showed me the bill. (Now this is where Master's surprising love shows)—the bill was for $601.00. That was the exact amount that Master had sent us through his visiting businessman angel!

We both thanked God, Christ, and Master. Our good friend from Seattle took us to our plane. Upon our return home, David went immediately into spinal surgery. Following that surgery, he healed quickly and perfectly. We were blessed with care and healing once again.

Something had been bothering me for years. I needed to have answers to a spiritual question that had been troubling me. Others have confirmed their need to know the answer, as well. Daya Ma was the one who could guide us. I gathered courage to reveal my self-doubt by asking questions regarding my spiritual progress. Of course I had read, meditated, and studied for many years, but I felt my progress was inadequate. Even though I meditated, served God, Christ, and guru, and worked at being the best person I could be, I felt that it was just not enough. Many times devotees have revealed the same feelings regarding self-doubt. It was time to ask for help.

I expressed my feelings to Daya Ma in a letter. I hoped she could help me and the others who found themselves in the same position. I asked her to give needed words of guidance and encouragement.

Her most welcome reply arrived and her sweet grace encouraged me. She reminded me that spiritual progress is not necessarily achieved by large numbers of Kriyas or by occurrences during meditation. She said that we must be patient with ourselves and our efforts to change and always broadcast love to God in our hearts. Also, we must trust in God's

Mary Peck Stockton

blessings for us.

She went on to say that every person is different. God's help depends on our personal particular needs for our soul's progress as we grow in meditation. Although we sometimes do not see tangible evidence of His help, He is always there. Our efforts give us results in the transformation of our consciousness. Results are sometimes intangible but real, and are forever beneficial. They may only be measured by their peace-giving qualities. Peace and a sense of well being are a response from God.

Daya Ma tells us that it is best that we do not try to compare our spiritual progress with others. We must concentrate on what we can do to deepen our own meditations and practice of Master's teachings. She told me that God sees the heart of a person and blesses the sincere devotee; also, that we need not be discouraged or feel inadequate. We need to understand that spiritual progress comes gradually, and that we must not analyze, or judge ourselves. We must just give and keep giving. She said as we sincerely do this in a heartfelt manner, God will respond.

Daya Ma urged us to understand that it is a spiritual law that when you make a sincere effort, you will know beyond doubt that you are progressing. If you do not give up, you will not fail. Never think you are unworthy. Daya Ma told us how very important it is to realize that God loves you just as you are and wants you to keep doing your part. He will help you, if you but ask. When we think we are unworthy, we are really absorbed within ourselves. But if we lose that little self and love God as our offering to Him, then all negative feelings will flee. Finally, she told me you will be assured that you are His child. As you pray, study, and meditate, know that Master will help you see the need to change yourself and grow according to God's plan for you. You will feel His love and joy.

These beautiful words paraphrased from Daya Ma have helped me establish peace in my soul regarding my spiritual progress. I pass them along to you, dear reader, in the hope they give you comfort and direction.

The picture of Master that touches my heart most deeply is the one titled "The Last Smile." That is how I remember him. In his eyes, I see love, sympathy, and compassion. Those eyes speak to me, comfort me, and encourage me. I even see those beautiful, deep eyes well up in tears as though he's saying to me, "Your hurt touches me deeply and I cry at the thought you must suffer." When I have a need to see him, I return to that picture, look directly into his eyes, and talk to him. That moment brings me once again in memory to stand in front of his living presence. From that picture—from his overpowering love—I receive the answers I am seeking.

CHAPTER EIGHT

Whispers from Master

~

The following guidelines were given me through intuitional insight and were received as answered prayer. I have collected these statements over a period of 25 years. They guided and helped me through problems, and have clarified my understanding throughout my lifetime. I pass them on to you so that you may find direction or comfort from them.

- I am responsible for my own stability and responses—no one else's.
- Stress means there is a pull or pulling to change something you are resisting. Examine it, learn to "give" or "change"—then do so. No longer will stress remain.
- Make sure that another person's encounter with you is one of Joy and Heaven—not Hell and Despair.
- Choose peace over pain.
- Courage is not the absence of fear. It's doing what it takes despite one's fear.
- It is I who must take command of myself to reach God—in prayer, in study, in daily living ... no one can do this for me. I cannot blame others or expect others to grow my soul for me.
- Offer the gift of yourself to others in peace and love.

If the gift is refused accept that in peace and love and be absolved of it—choose peace.

- That which we send, we receive. Broadcast love and peace and receive it.

- If we allow God's spirit to work through our minds, words, and actions, we can't help but love one another ... because He is love.

- Love yourself! Don't be in agreement with those who don't care about you. Be in harmony and agreement with God, Jesus, Paramahansa Yogananda, and all of the gurus who do love you.

- Let no one manipulate you against God's will.

- Take charge; God gave you free will—use it. Take charge of your life, your emotions, your actions. God will give you the go-ahead.

- What I do today will affect who I am tomorrow, and all of the future tomorrows.

- We must not condemn our brothers, for if we do, we are pointing out what it is in us that needs healing. We see others' faults that have a basis in ourselves. To condemn faults in others is to fortify faults in ourselves. If we love others, and do not condemn, we are loving them as God loves us, and we are free from that condemnation ourselves. Let God's Spirit in us love all others with His perfect love.

- You can determine your spiritual vibration by watching others' reactions to you—they more surely, kindly, lovingly, respectfully respond to the God that they see in you.

- A flower doesn't grow if you smother its seed. Human beings are the same.
- Are you guiding or forcefully pushing your children?
- Where there is no love and trust, there is fear.
- We create our own faults; how can we blame others for the fruits of them?
- "Taking charge" does not mean you are a controlling person: people who won't, can't, or don't are threatened by people who will, can, and do.
- We must fight ignorance, for that is our enemy — not each other.
- Living without God as your polestar is like being a straw battered by a stormy ocean wave.
- A strong mind is a wonderful thing to have—as long as it is balanced with fairness and compassion.
- Don't be a stick-in-the-mud: become a wavelet on the flowing river of love.
- When you "connect" with Almighty Spirit, ask for every need. Even ordinary things will be given to you—if you but ask for help.
- Think about this: What goes into your mouth and comes out of it determines what kind of person you become. This can mean words or food.
- Life goes full circle. As a child you are to be "seen and not heard." Youth and midlife become ego and ma-

terial satisfaction. In old age you return to being seen, not heard; and, sometimes, old people are not even seen. God sees and hears us through our entire lifetime.

- Praying is like eating fruits and vegetables. If you don't go to the store, pick them up, pay for them, and eat them, they won't be able to nourish you—prayer is like that. You must sit down, talk to God, tell Him/Her what you need and want—then He can help you. Therefore, you must do your part, or nothing can help you.

- There are two sides to everything. Your body, your brain, and two sides to each argument or thought—good or bad. You must live in balance between all.

- Learn to let go. We are hanging on a precipice of fear by our fingertips. Master comes and releases them one-by-one until we let go entirely, and plunge into God's love and care.

- Dying is falling *into* love (God is love).

- Relax—you can't complete anything in life or life itself. It is never ending.

- Some people, like flowers, are so beautiful that we can't believe they are real. We must reach out spiritually and touch them to be one with them; to know their truth, and that is you ... my flower, my friend.

- If you want a tree to stand and grow—you don't keep hitting it with an axe.

Mary Peck Stockton

- Anything that is painful is not lasting.
- Dress your soul in God's light. Then you will be perfectly dressed forever!
- I don't want to *improve* my bad habits—I want to *remove* them.
- You say you are following Jesus. But are you riding in the second bus?
- Precious memories, like roses, are beautiful to see; but none of them have fragrance without Spirit in me.
- Let me give rose petals of love in return for the harm given me.
- You can control no one in life but yourself—when you do that, you'll see that you don't need to control others.
- Memories that must be forgiven—hurtful moments—all belong to God. Let them go!
- I will be healed when I stop yielding to evil.
- You say you are having a "bad hair day "—well, don't forget, it goes the way you brush it!
- The world is being run by a bunch of "errorists"—not "terrorists."
- Life is imperfection heading toward God, who is everlasting perfection.
- A character blemish is not a blemish—it's an eruption of a need. It can only be cleansed wholly by His love and direction.
- God's love is more powerful than my fears.

- I will cry and try until you ply your boat for me.
- He and only He can fill my soul with peace.
- The cup of life will not be filled unless I can pour right living in.
- At both ends of life you get "growing pains" (tests and trials).
- Deep prayers are like paying taxes: A small amount goes to the greater good for all to improve.
- Satan drives us—God leads us.
- If you believe you are sick, you will be sick. If you believe you are weak, so shall you be. If you believe you are well and strong, that shall come about.
- Enjoy the beauty of the present season—don't be drowned by the ashes of past sad memories.
- An incomplete pass doesn't win a ball game; complete your life with meditation: Win the game of life.
- "Senior moments" may be God's way of interrupting that which you probably shouldn't say anyway. It seems that God taps us on the shoulder saying, "Hold it," until the right time.
- Life is a test—I hope I do all right in the finals!
- Life isn't wishing—it's working!
- Don't worry about having a face lift—concentrate on a soul lift.
- Be a beacon of God's light—let Him shine through you. Always give a smile; you may never know how deeply you touch someone's soul with a smile. It

doesn't cost you a penny, but it gives riches to those who see it.

- It doesn't matter who you were in a previous life, but it matters very much what you do in this life. Time is growing shorter daily, so work hard for your soul growth. You are the only one who can do the work. With Master at your right hand, you can grow into paradise.

- God gave us a variety of voices to form a chorus of souls. He didn't want just a lot of soloists—so cooperate!

- God is the essence of my being. Without Him, I can't exist. You must have patience to achieve what you ask from God—He doesn't use a watch.

- When you think you can't make it up a hill (trials), put yourself in (or shift into) "God-gear."

- The same wall that keeps people from coming in keeps you from going out.

- Wrinkles are railroad tracks that prepare you for the trip to eternity.

- To the extent that one lifts himself in love, peace, goodness, mercy, kindness, and understanding, it will elevate that person to that degree spiritually. Therefore, in prayer, you should strive to reach as high as you can.

- —— (Name) is living in a different thought world.
  — (Name) is a beloved child of God. Don't try to force

a change in —— (Name). Change yourself to understand his needs.

- What I see in others that annoys me, God is showing me in that person, so I may view that which I must change in myself.

CHAPTER NINE

Poetry and Prayers

⌒ω

Have I Disappointed or Let You Down?

(poem received as a response to my prayer)

Good work thou brave and gentle soul –
Mild and meek, but warrior for truth untold.
A banner, then became a sword
To love, cherish, and stand for our Lord.

Tune into His word for pathways bright,
And know He is here—both day and night.
Rest well, sweet soul, for you I love …
Your heart is mine and will be above.

The Final Performance
(a reverie written January 27, 1997)

Backstage, I await the stage director's cue. I am a bit nervous as I view the final stage of "death." I wonder at the reception that awaits me, but when the chorus of angels' music swells, I know I must go ... on.

I walk on stage bathed in light, wearing a gossamer gown of radiant hue. My hair flows down my back in a cascade of love. I am held in the embrace of the loving spirit from the audience of souls who wish me well.

I give my last performance with all my heart to this earth's stage. The swelling chorus of angels—the heavenly choir—supports me with love and prayers. When my last breath has been expended, and my last loving note sung, the final curtain begins to close.

At last, my performance is done. I take my final bow. I go to give my encore to Him alone ... to my God! I turn and face the "Director"—the one to whom I give my trust and hand. He leads me off "death stage" to enter the "New Theatre of Life."

Easter 1985

A cross was raised,

A man was hung,

A rose was born.

My beautiful rose—perfect flower from God—born of thorns and mud-raised in your full beauty above all mankind; let your beauty be in my heart forever. Let the wafted incense of your overpowering sweetness guide me home forever. I love you Jesus. Cover me with your petals of love—bring me home to your beauty—lasting and forever.

Dear God,

Be with me in my pain; envelop me with Your love and even *become* the pain. Then may I accept my trials and be grateful.

Dear God,

Make me one with You to experience all things through You, so that I may always be *one in You.*

Dear God,

Remove from me the embedded "dark crystal" in my soul—pulverize it with Thy Holy Light. Replace it with the "clear crystal" of Your Love and Light.

Dear God,

Keep me in Thy Presence, Lord—that I may forego and *forgive* the past.

Dear God,

Teach us to be truly mature in our love for You. Help us be sympathetic, to be more understanding and thoughtful of others. Help us to refrain from criticism of others. We have no right to pass judgement on one another. You, God alone, have that right. Help us to be humble, so that we may have a sweetly secret, silent, loving relationship with You. Give me true humility so I may certainly know that, Lord, You are the doer, not I. Bless us in our efforts to love with a true and mature love.

Dear God,

Become with me so strongly that I know You everywhere and forever.

Dear God,

Bring peace to whomever I see, that they may know You through me.

CHAPTER TEN

Conclusion

Mary Peck Stockton

When my mother first met Master, he told her that she, my brother, and I would always be cared for and guided. These words stayed with us and were proven again and again as we emerged victoriously from our many trials. I have felt Master's hand guiding and protecting me through every difficult situation. As I spiritually hold onto his strong hand, I receive his loving guidance that directs and supports me through every obstacle.

Life experiences carried me away from deep and steady contact with the teachings in my twenties and thirties. I felt, as always, that I was cared for, that I could cruise through the rest of my life secure in Master's promise of love and guidance. Mind you, I *never* left His presence, but I didn't do my homework to make myself receptive to the gifts and love I could have received.

Many tests and temptations during that time taught me that I must do *my* part. When I finally re-connected with SRF, Daya Ma's written question to me was why they had not heard from me. My answer to her was that I was traveling through many deep test chasms and circumstances. I felt, through them all, that I was cared for and loved.

At this juncture in my life, a dramatic change took place

in me—I left my material leanings and headed for an anchor in my spiritual home. Master had kept calling me through those tests of mine. When I came "home" to deep meditation practice and study, I felt like the prodigal child returning to my spiritual life anew.

The tests never stopped, but throughout them all, I received the constant tugging at my soul to enter and re-enter the *real* world of spiritual assurance through deep meditation and right living. I plan to *never* leave those blessed shores.

All the years of Master's watching and caring for me have culminated in the writing of this book—an event of true love. The purpose of this entire book is to show you, dear reader, that his words are true. All of Master's spiritual family can receive the same grace.

Throughout my lifetime, one thread runs clear and strong: I am cared for. I will emerge from trials with victory, strength, added courage, and understanding. God loves everyone equally and, with your faith, He will grace you with His love.

During the writing of this book, I began to experience major pains in the area of my previous colon cancer. After four days of extreme discomfort, I was advised by my clinic to go to the hospital emergency room. The doctor there took tests and x-rays, and I was told to return to my primary doctor for further instruction. I did so immediately. She recommended that I have a colonoscopy as soon as possible. In the meantime, instructions were given to me by the emergency room doctor to treat the immediate problem with remedies that he supplied. For the severe pain caused by the blockage, I was provided a prescription of morphine, to be used at my discretion. I did not need the drug, as my meditations supplied a release from pain.

I kept urgently requesting a release from the doctor so that I could fulfill my assigned role as the Kriya registrar for the SRF Tour 2000 scheduled in Portland. The meeting was to be held within a few days of my emergency room experience. I wanted so very much to serve our Guru and SRF. This was not to be!

As I sat in the emergency room with my husband, he quietly said, "Let it go, Mary, let it go." Finally, after five hours of tests and attempts at hurrying the healing process, I surrendered. Upon returning home from the hospital, I was convinced that I must let go and let God. I was replaced at Tour 2000 and was assured that the position I had been assigned could be filled by someone else.

Friends from Seattle had planned to meet me at Tour 2000. I called them and told them of my plight, but said that I would try to meet with them for a couple of hours. A meditation was held at the Portland Center the night before the beginning of Tour 2000. Brahmachari Kirk had asked for special prayers for my recovery as the group meditated together. I felt the comforting prayers being sent, and my pain began to subside somewhat. By the time of the last day of the retreat, I was able to dress and go to the hotel to meet with my friends.

When I arrived at the hotel, I was greeted with such love and compassion that I was overwhelmed! A darling little girl, Rose, greeted me with a handful of roses. Later, the church members from the Portland Center who planned the retreat gave me the flowers that were used in the Kriya ceremony. The garland of white carnations with red roses that had graced Master's picture was breathtaking. Also, the beautiful centerpiece was given me, and both are presently in front of me on the table as I write.

I attended the last day presentation of the film *Glimpses of a Life Divine*. It was like seeing my life with Master all over again as the film covered his progress in America from 1924 on. I had participated in many of the scenes that I saw in the film. It was very difficult to hold back the tears of fond remembrances.

One of the members of the Seattle Center died of colon cancer recently. His widow was among those who met with me. As we sat in the lobby of the hotel, these words from Master (previously given to me) came to me intuitively: "Dying is falling *into* love." This touched her deeply as I told her the message from Master. Upon leaving, she presented me a picture of her beloved one. (When I got back home, his picture was placed in front of the centerpiece of flowers on my "Kriya" table, and I said a prayer for his beautiful soul.)

As time came for me to leave the retreat, and as the group said its farewells, Master's love surrounded us all. That same deep, pure, abiding love came from every heart I saw that day. Brahmachari Kirk and Brother Naradananda seemed to embrace everyone's love. It was passed directly to my heart. There were not many dry eyes around us as we left the meeting place. Everyone assured me of continuing prayers and love.

My daughter arrived at the hotel to pick us up, I eagerly told her of all the wondrous love I had received. Her response was that after all the years of hardship and hurt I'd suffered, God, Christ, and Guru were now surrounding me with all the healing love I'd missed. Through that love extended to me from everyone, I was assured of God's ever-present help, hope, and people's supporting "feathers" of prayer in my final years.

During this varied life of mine, I have been blessed to be reacquainted with souls who have been virtual sons and daughters to me. Perhaps they have come through their need of spiritual communication, or to be with one who could understand, appreciate, and guide them. They have proven to be spiritual companions of love and help in my life's journey. Regardless of who they are or what their present background, we connect at the spiritual level and both are helped by it. We have been brought together in times of need, and it is apparent to me that it is all a part of Master's plan. Our scenario has been written—our way has been taught. It is now for us to recognize, receive, open our hearts, and pray for each other as we work on our spiritual advancement.

It is imperative for me to clearly state the fact that Master's lessons, love, and wisdom have seen me through all difficult and good times. His presence has never left me. He exists in my life's realities now even more than when I knew him in the body. He has promised that he will do the same for all who accept him as their true guru. He is able to help more people now that he is not body-bound.

Recently, as I was meditating, a very strong intuitive message was received that must be included in this book. The message was in regard to prayer and meditation. The words given were:

"Don't give up. You can't know where you are on the spiritual ladder. You may need only one more step to reach the glorious goal. You may be only a few Kriya repetitions from reaching maximum happiness. Only God knows where your past karma has put you. Keep on working. You are *assured* of success. All efforts will be positively counted in your next step of spiritual evolution. As a householder, you may not be able to meditate twelve hours, but I want to tell you that *any* meditation time will help you."

My closing words to you are never lose heart and don't let doubt enter your mind. He is here—he is helping you, and me, and our loved ones constantly. All he asks is loyalty, and that you meditate and ask for help. It shall be given!

Aum, Shanti, Aum

Addenda

Addendum A

Heavenly Visit with Daya Mata

February 15, 1996

Mary Peck Stockton and her daughter, Mary Caroline Williver

Mary Caroline and I arrived at Mt. Washington about one-and-a-half hours early. We were so eager to see Daya Mata that we wanted to be certain that we'd not miss our scheduled appointment time. Flowers we had brought to present to Daya Ma were handed to the receptionist for safe-keeping until we were allowed to go upstairs for the visit.

Sister Namita, Daya Ma's personal secretary, came down-stairs to greet us. Since we were early, she graciously offered to take us on a tour of the grounds. We followed her out the main doors. She began to point out the new buildings and their expanded offices, as well as the nuns' quarters. I ques-tioned the safety of the buildings because they were built on a steep hillside. She explained that they were built like a fortress against any eventuality. The grounds and buildings were so lovely and well-kept. It was hard to realize that I'd walked these very grounds almost fifty years ago.

We visited Master's wishing well. It had been enshrined since I first saw it. I remember the day my mother and I had the privilege of taking a tour of the grounds with Master, himself, as our tour guide. He seemed especially delighted to show us his treasured wishing well.

When we returned to the main building with Sister Namita, the receptionist served us apple juice in the library. We showed Sister Namita some of my mother's collection of SRF materials. We chatted about the "old days" for awhile. Mary and I were invited to make ourselves comfortable as Sister Namita excused herself to go on with her duties.

Mary and I went into the large auditorium where I had attended Kriya ceremonies three times. Master himself had conducted the first two services. The third was offered by Brother Anandamoy. I sat down and began to quietly reminisce about the times I had participated in the Kriya ceremonies there.

Looking back in memory, when I attended the last Kriya, I had been accompanied by my mother. We drove from Riverside to Los Angeles to attend the service. I recalled how, during the ceremony, Brother Anandamoy stood in front of us scattering rose petals. It seemed he extended his time at our row of chairs as a handful of rose petals was directed at me. When I returned home from that trip, I learned of my cancer. I wondered at the time if Master had directed Brother Anandamoy to give me a special blessing.

Mary brought me back from my reverie by announcing

that she wanted to move our car from the side parking lot to the front of the building. I returned to the library. She joined me once again in the library as Sister Namita came to tell us that Daya Ma was running late. I said, "I've waited forty-six years; a few minutes makes no difference!"

In a short time, the receptionist who'd been caring for our flowers handed them to us and told us our wait would not be much longer. Sister Namita then came to direct us up three flights of stairs. She offered us the opportunity to ride in the elevator, but we declined because we felt we were in need of exercise.

We were guided to Daya Ma's reception area. She was sitting in her small living room. She sat in the west corner— her chair was placed between two windows. The Pacific Ocean was easily visible from those windows. Wearing big smiles, we approached Daya Ma and pranamed to her. I handed her the flowers, which she graciously received. Her first words were, "I've been waiting years to see you." She invited us to lean over and receive a big hug. She smiled sweetly at Mary as I introduced the two, and I noticed that Mary was sparkling like fireworks, which she continued to do throughout the entire visit.

We began conversing as though I had been there just yesterday. We both recalled old times with Master. I showed her my mother's copies of Paramahansa Yogananda's 1930 lessons, his 1926 outlines, and a personal noted from Jane, a friend of my mother. She told me Jane's SRF name and said she was now in retirement.

I reported some of my life's happenings. We discussed my marriage to David, and we all laughed when I explained to Daya Ma how Mary had "wheedled" David into our lives by offering to clean his house if he'd come to dinner.

I told Daya Ma that, since I lived so far away from my mother in her later years, Mary had become her ambassador for care. Daya Ma asked Mary if she was married and Mary replied in the affirmative. I could sense that Daya Ma was pleased with Mary's beautiful soul.

As I was showing Daya Ma the SRF materials from my mother's collection, I told her that I had planned to donate a group of these to be displayed at the Seattle church. She was delighted and said that she does miss traveling to the centers, and that she'd love to visit all of us. I told her how loving the SRF group in Seattle is and she said, "Oh, I know it."

I shared my spiritual hospital experience with Daya Ma and she asked me to write about it and send a copy to her. She told me she'd had an experience as well in the past, but she hadn't told Master about it until the year before he passed on. Out of respect for her privacy, I didn't question her further.

I told Daya Ma that during my experience Master had guided me upward through many levels and I saw people living in a variety of situations. I questioned her about why I keep seeing these people during my meditations. She replied that I have been with Master many times, and that these are people I knew in my past life. I asked why I had to be confronted with the frightening vision that preceded the entire experience. She told me there was something I needed to change in my spirit. I told her I knew that it was unforgiveness. As Master guided me upward, he informed me of my need to change before I finally returned to God. I told Daya Ma that for the previous thirteen years, I have systematically called, written, or prayed giving forgiveness to those I'd not forgiven, and that I also asked forgiveness from those I'd hurt. She smiled and said that was good.

Daya Ma told us that she was writing a book about the Second Coming of Christ, as well as another book. She told us she goes into seclusion to write, just as did Master when he was writing. I told her I remember his need to retreat in order to write.

We then discussed Mary's candy and nut business. At the mention of candy, Daya Ma's face lighted up. She said, "Do you make it? I love chocolate. What kind is it?" Mary answered that she made English toffee and promised that she would bring some to her. That pleased Daya Ma, and thrilled me that Mary could be of service to her.

I began to show Daya Ma the psychological profile outline gleaned from my mother's collection of Master's materials. I informed her I had become a psychologist. She said that she had always been interested in psychology. She then reiterated that she knew that I'd been with Master many,

many times, and that he was using me for his work.

At that point in our conversation, she told me some disciples are writing their memories of Paramahansa Yogananda. She was pleased when I told her I had already written some papers about my days with Master. I told her I had sent her a copy and asked if she'd had a chance to read it. She said no, but she indicated she would send for it right away and read it. I told her much of the material came to me intuitively in the late night hours and the early hours of the day, and that I certainly felt it was Master guiding me as I wrote. She repeated that he was working through me. I told her that those who read my writings expressed their gratitude and told me that it had helped them through difficult times.

I felt compelled to bring up a subject that had bothered me for many years. When I last saw Master, I didn't pranam to him. I don't know why I didn't. Maybe I was spellbound by his presence, but I did not pay proper homage to him with a pranam. I'm sure he has forgiven me, but I asked her to please tell him I was sorry about my impropriety. She told me, "Tell him yourself. Go into his room, meditate, and talk to him." She immediately called Sister Namita and asked her to take Mary and me into Master's private quarters, bring us chairs, and let us meditate. My heart began to beat so fast at the prospect of being in his rooms that I thought it might stop.

Before we left to meditate, Sister Namita handed Daya

Ma two books. Daya Ma inscribed in one for Mary and in the other for me. They were her books titled *Finding the Joy Within* and *Only Love*. We thanked her and I said, "You are so beautiful." She handed me a long wrapped gift in green paper (a sandalwood letter opener and a heart-shaped, decorated incense burner). She told me that these gifts were for my husband. She then asked me to come back and see her again, and to be sure to bring David the next time. She suggested that we could stay at the Lake Shrine when we came back to see her.

As Mary and I got up from our chairs, a blustery storm came over the area, blowing heavy winds and rain. The windows banged open and shut, but Daya Ma and I didn't react. Sister Namita came in quickly to close the window. Daya Ma and I kept looking deeply into each other's eyes.

As we began to leave, I remembered I had brought a "throw away" camera so that we could take pictures of Daya Ma. She showed an interest in the camera and said she'd not seen one like that before. We were given permission to take a picture if we sent her a copy. I requested that Sister Namita take pictures of Daya Ma, Mary, and me.

Mary and I kneeled at Daya Ma's feet. As I was getting up, Daya Ma pulled me down close to her and kissed and hugged me. I stroked her cheek softly with my right hand, looked deeply into her eyes, and said, "I love you." She told me that I was beautiful and that she loved me, too. I then sincerely thanked her for everything, and in those few words she, I'm sure, understood that I was thanking her and Master for all the years of help and love I'd received. We drank in that moment of God's loving presence. It was time now for Mary and me to meditate. We felt so very honored that we were allowed to go to Master's quarters to pray. We said goodbye and followed Sister Namita out of the room.

Master's quarters were down the hall from Daya Ma's reception room. As we went to the door to enter his rooms, we removed our shoes. There were white cotton runners on the floor and all chairs were covered with white cloth. A nun brought a chair for each of us. Mary placed her chair in front of Master's overstuffed chair in his sitting room. He was sitting in that chair when I saw him last in 1950. I took my chair into his bedroom. There, I positioned myself next to his bed. His bed was regular size with a carved wood headboard. I sat quietly drinking in the wonder of the moment and realizing where I was blessed to be. A youthful picture of Master in meditation was centered on the bed. The head of the bed was positioned to the east. Master's personal possessions were laid about the room. Pictures of his Gurus: Sri Yukteswar, Babaji, and Lahiri Mahasaya were framed and placed on the walls.

On a chair next to a table, I saw the carved wooden box into which requests for prayers are placed. It is there, Daya Ma told me, that she meditates and prays for those people whose names are placed in the box. I sat quietly by Master's bed, meditated, and asked his forgiveness. I then spoke qui-

Mary Peck Stockton

etly to him of my need to apologize for my youthful over-sight many years before. I felt peace descend upon me as I expressed myself sincerely. What a wonderful blessing I was given to be in his room.

Master's quarters were quite the same as they were when I had visited him in 1950; it seemed the furniture was left untouched. Memories of the past rushed through my mind as I absorbed the wonder of being where we were. Mary and I were surely blessed to be given the opportunity to meditate at Master's feet where he had actually stood.

After our meditation, Mary and I got up and carried our chairs out into the hallway. A nun accompanied us as we were directed to the descending stairway. I looked back in the direction of Daya Ma's sitting room. She was now bless-ing a small child. The little girl was accompanied by her father. I waved and threw Daya Ma a kiss that she returned to me with a big smile. I waved and silently said, "Thank you and goodbye." What a wonderful memory to always carry in my heart.

As I descended the stairway, I felt such joy and peace. We went to our car and drove down the mountain in joyous conversation about the wonderful experience we had just been privileged to live. We were so happy! We realized we had spent an hour as close to heaven as this world offers.

I would be negligent if I did not describe Daya Ma more thoroughly so that you can envision her. I noted that her skin was very soft and smooth. Her hair is all white now—

her eyes peaceful, quiet, and very blue. She was adorned in a lovely saffron colored sari that complemented her beautiful complexion. At all times, she sat straight. Her peaceful countenance put both of us at ease immediately—her love was all encompassing.

To honor her request, my husband and I returned to visit Daya Ma. The account of my husband's impressions of that visit will be found in Addendum B. Also, my impressions will be found in Addendum C.

ADDENDUM B

October 6, 1996

Re: Notes and Impressions from Visit with Daya Mata.

Where: Mt. Washington—SRF International Headquarters

When: September 19, 1996

         (length of meeting—45 minutes)

Present: Sri Daya Mata, Mary A. Stockton,

         Sister Namita (personal secretary to Daya Mata),

         David A. Stockton

From: David A. Stockton

The time came for our visit with Daya Mata, and we met with Sister Namita, who escorted us to a room on the third floor of Headquarters. It was a bright and cheerful room filled with light from windows on two sides. There was a couch along one wall, and in the middle of the room stood a coffee table with a large vase filled to capacity with multicolored flowers. Daya Mata, adorned in a beautiful orange silk sari, was sitting at the back of the room; a smaller table with a second vase of colorful flowers was placed beside her. Indeed, a pretty and peaceful scene for the eyes and mind upon entering the room.

She waved a friendly welcome and kept smiling as Sister Namita led us across the room. We pranamed and joyful greetings were exchanged; in a few moments Daya Mata invited us to be seated on the couch.

She and Mary began immediately to catch up on the happenings and experiences since the last time they met. I noted Daya Mata's sense of calm and poise and that her bearing was dignified and regal; yet she projected an informal, relaxed, and unassuming attitude that at once put me at ease. Her eyes sparkled and were filled with love and compassion as the animated conversation continued. She was interested in hearing about our present work and our various activities.

We told her we had brought a photo book with greetings and pictures from the newly opened Seattle Center and she was very pleased. She asked us to come and sit by her side so we could share the pictures together. We crossed the room and sat on the floor beside her chair, adding more to the informal and relaxed atmosphere.

Mary handed her the photo album and Daya Mata placed it in her lap and began to slowly turn the pages. She was interested in all the pictures as she came to them, and she would pause at each one as we discussed its details. She remarked on the pictures that showed the windows of the new church and how beautiful the windows were—she mentioned this more than once. She was interested in the pictures of church members, especially those showing the volunteers working in various jobs getting the newly purchased church building ready for use.

She was pleased to read some writings that were included in the album. One was a message bringing greetings from the Seattle devotees written by the church's coordinator. Another was a poem I had written to commemorate the day of the first service in the new church. This led to a brief discussion about poetry, and I told her I enjoyed writing short poems at times. She said she used to write poetry, too. We found that we enjoyed reading and writing poems written in both free form and in meter and rhyme.

Sitting next to Daya Mata and sharing the contents of the album as she turned its pages, I became more aware of the quiet, calm feeling in the room. The windows were open and a gentle, cooling breeze was flowing throughout the room, tempering the heat from the afternoon sun. In stark contrast to the noise and traffic on the streets of Los Angeles below, the peace and tranquility enveloping this room at Headquarters on the top of Mt. Washington made it a world apart.

When Daya Mata finished looking through the book, Mary then presented her with nuts and candy that our daughter, Mary Caroline, had sent to her as a gift. Mary Caroline was also fulfilling a promise that she had made when she and her mother visited Daya Mata some months ago. She had discussed the nut and candy business with Daya Mata and had promised to see that she would receive some of each. Daya Mata was delighted to receive the nuts and candy and said how much she would enjoy them. Mary also gave her the blue carrying bag we brought them in and she was pleased to receive that. She, in return, presented us with a gift of a canned food made from gluten. (A description of this food, and an interesting story about it, is given in Mary's written account of our visit, under the title "Addendum C").

The photo album and the gifts were set aside, and Daya Mata and Mary began to talk of those they both had known in the early days in SRF. Daya Mata said she often thought of the people and the happenings and experiences of those times. It was a joy to see two such longtime friends look back in years together, and through their recollections, relive some cherished memories.

The conversation turned to Master's teachings and how they applied in everyday living. We discussed a number of these and, in particular, I recall what Daya Mata said about two of his teachings. One was that Master wanted people to be cheerful—he wanted them to be happy and to laugh and smile. He said that to live a God-centered life did not mean that one had to go around in a somber manner with a long face—one should be joyous, reflecting a positive attitude.

The other teaching we discussed regarded the importance of meditation. Daya Mata stressed the importance of having made meditation a daily habit. She emphasized that she never fails to meditate, no matter how tired she might

Mary Peck Stockton

be. Daya Mata reiterated that daily meditation is now an ingrained habit in her life—it is something she does without fail.

The talk then turned to her speech given at the 1996 convocation, and how she had no idea of what she was going to say before starting to speak. She said that the words were given to her by Master as she spoke; they came forth freely without any thought on her part, and that the words were amusing and brought laughter. She was amazed and pleased at how the entire audience laughed. Usually, she said, only a small part of an audience laughs at something humorous, but this time it appeared that everybody was laughing.

The subject of our new Seattle church was brought up again, and she was glad about its progress. She said she would so much like to visit everyone there. Mary told her about plans for an open house and that the devotees hoped that someone from Headquarters could come to speak at the service and view the church. Daya Mata called to Sister Namita to join us. When she came, Daya Mata asked Sister Namita to remind her that somebody be sent from Headquarters to be present at the open house.

It was now time to leave and we said our good-byes; Sister Namita escorted us to the elevator. With a young nun as the operator, the elevator returned us to the first floor. We took a last look at the displays in the large entry and walked outside.

We got into our car and began the drive back down the

mountain. I thought back over the wonderful events of the past hours—memories that will remain with me for the rest of my life.

It was a cherished time that I shall never forget. I consider it an honor and a privilege that I was allowed to be a part of such a sacred visit. Being in her presence and being able to visit with Daya Mata was a once-in-a-lifetime happening that will remain a highlight of my life.

✌

ADDENDUM C

This visit with Sri Daya Mata was held on September 19, 1996 at Mt. Washington SRF International Headquarters. Present were Sri Daya Mata, David A. Stockton, Mary A. Stockton, and Sister Namita, personal secretary to Sri Daya Mata.

Daya Mata received David and me in her private sitting room. She looked radiantly beautiful, as she greeted us with a warm smile. Her hair, now white, was neatly arranged softly around her face. As David and I pranamed to her, she opened her arms to envelop me and allowed a kiss on the cheek.

As we embraced, she said, "I saw you only awhile ago." I answered that it had been eight months since my daughter, Mary Caroline, and I had visited. I told her I was keeping my promise given at that time to bring my husband, David, to meet her. I then introduced him to her. We were invited to make ourselves comfortable and we sat on a nearby couch.

After a short time, we moved to sit on the floor at Daya Ma's feet since we had brought items to share with her. We presented her with a photo album that contained a loving letter from the Seattle Center devotees. In that album, also, were pictures of the center, as well as group and action pictures of devotees who had worked so diligently to make the center available for SRF activities. Included in the album was a poem that David had written about the opening day of the center.

Daya Ma graciously received the gift. I told her that the album itself had been gleaned from my mother's possessions after she had died. Therefore, we considered the album to be a gift from her. That pleased Daya Ma, as she and my mother had a long term loving friendship.

Sri Daya Ma said she was very pleased with the devotees' dedication that produced such a beautiful center.

She began to recall early times with Master and told us of the cooperative efforts and activities that brought the present temples into being. We reminisced about people, dates, and the activities of our early organization. While recalling the past, I relayed a loving message of "hello" from Marjorie Profitt who, with her husband, helped build the wall at Encinitas under the direction of Master. Her husband became the first lay minister at SRF. Daya Ma just beamed as we relived old times and recalled people connected to the activities. Daya Ma said she used to watch for my mother and me every week as we attended services. She said certain people stand out in a group and that she always noted our presence.

David and I carried many messages and gifts from our

Seattle devotees; also, various questions posed by members. While answering, Daya Ma sat up and became full of visible light and energy, obviously guided by Master. I felt that he was speaking through her.

A question was posed by a Seattle devotee regarding going deeper in meditation. Daya Ma said that Master had told Rajarsi not to be restless nor discouraged. Also, that *regularity* — the habit of meditation is the *most important*. When you are tired, habit is the most important. Daya Ma said that many times she was very tired, but her habit of meditation always carried her on to meditate. She went on to say that *repetition becomes habit*; it is not just techniques that are important. It is *techniques plus devotion*. She urged all to give God love. God is the source of love; you must open your heart to Him.

Daya Ma told us that the term "Mother God" was coined by Master. She stated that many religions are now recognizing God as Mother. She urged devotees to talk to Him/Her as we would a loving parent.

Responding to our remarks about the audience at the 1996 Convocation loving her speech, she said she had prepared no speech. Instead, she went into Master's quarters to be still and receive his guidance before going to the meeting. She reiterated that she made no speech preparation. She said it was all Master speaking and that he was speaking with great humor.

As she told us about this, she straightened and became

very animated and happy. She said that she had the whole audience laughing—usually there are only one or two hundred that laugh, but everyone was laughing hard. She told us it was wonderful; it was as Master always did—he liked to make people laugh.

We presented our daughter's candy that was sent to fulfill an earlier promise to Daya Ma. Also, members from the Seattle Center had sent gifts and these we carried to her in a turquoise-blue silk tote. I asked her if she'd like to keep the tote and she answered, "Oh, may I have it? I love it."

She handed me a gift, a can of Worthington Vegetarian Skallops (a vegetable and grain product). She said that these are used in many ways at Headquarters. She recalled the times when Master had served gluten products to his ashram people in Ranchi in 1918. Years later, at Headquarters, Master asked her and the nuns to wash and wash flour until it was without starch—all that remained was gluten. From that they prepared loaves and patties that were served in many ways.

Daya Ma then presented us with a 1997 SRF picture calendar on which she wrote: "To Mary and David—such a joy to see you here at Mother Center. God bless you. Divine love, Daya Mata, 9/19/96." This gift shall be cherished forever.

Daya Ma responded to specific questions sent by Seattle members. David and I both took notes so that we could carry the messages back to them. She reiterated how much she would love to visit us all. She remarked about the beautiful church windows made by a Seattle devotee and expressed her appreciation of them.

I told her I had planned to donate my mother's collection of Master's notes, personal letters, early lessons, and other materials to the center. These would be put on display for the members to enjoy. That plan seemed to please her very much.

Time was fleeting, but Daya Ma gave no indication of tiring. However, I sensed that our visit of love and joy should soon come to an end. We did not want to impose on her grace for too long a time. Forty-five minutes had passed as though it were just five minutes.

We asked her permission to take a picture with us. She said yes, but only under the condition that we send her a copy. She called Sister Namita in to take the photos. We remained positioned at her feet and beamed as much as we could. We, of course, have sent the promised photos to her.

We made a request for a speaker to come to the Seattle Center, which was granted immediately. She asked Sister Namita to arrange for a speaker right away. By the time we returned to Seattle, dates for the speaker had already been arranged. The dates were November 8, 9, and 10, 1996.

We thanked Daya Ma for her gracious visit with us. We departed her loving presence with joy and happiness in our hearts. As we were leaving, Sister Namita told us that Daya Ma was pleased to see us, and that she is seeing very few people now because of her heavy schedule. Needless to say, we felt very honored to have been granted our lovely visit.

The memories of the times spent with Master and Daya Ma shall never leave my heart. I feel so very blessed to know two of the most beautiful souls ever born to this earth.

~

ADDENDUM D

(This account was written by my mother, Mrs. Mary Peck, describing the last time she was privileged to be in Master's presence.)

Mrs. Mary Peck
3880 San Rafael
Los Angeles 65, California

January 10, 1951
Wednesday, about 2:30 p.m.

I saw P.Y. then on the third floor of Mt. Washington about 2:30 p.m. during meditation period. Jeanette and I saw Master Paramhansa Yogananda, our Guruji, in the hall in the wheel chair pushed by Mrs. M. Lewis, Dr. M. Lewis' wife, and Durga (Mrs. Darling). We greeted Guruji and said, "how happy we were to see him, that everyone loved him." He had mangoes in his lap and 2 crisp $1.00 bills in his hand.

He gave one dollar to Jeanette and one to me. He also gave a mango to Jeanette and one to me. I cannot express my innermost joy at seeing Guruji again and he said, "It's been a long time, at last you are here—I waited for you a long time." [I recalled the first time when we met in 1931 in San Diego at the Sun Room in the San Diego Hotel, where classes were held. He called me out of the line—that is, asked me to remain after the others had left, and asked, "if I would like to join the work?" I explained my situation—home, husband, and the children were small. My father and mother were here visiting with us from Philadelphia, Pa., also. Then Guruji said, "well, later on."] So here the time arrived.

Yesterday, Faye Wright told Guruji that I had been sick with a cold last week and he replied, "oh my goodness!" Today, he called for me to come up and I am so glad as it was another prayer answered. I sent out a thought last night to have Guruji send for me to see him and it came to pass sooner than I dreamed. Guruji added, "you look much better than you did before," and said, "I always called you and your daughter sisters," and he laughed just like a very pleased child after his wish was fulfilled. He said, "see, things turned out all right didn't they?" I replied, "yes, if it had not been for your prayers and help we would not be here today—we had a new birth." He then mentioned the closeness of the great danger we had at home in the past. I thanked him again and he blessed Jeanette and I. He talked with her for awhile also. Then, two of the men brought up a birthday gift for Guruji, a deck table. They demonstrated it in the hall. Guruji kept talking to us anyway, no matter what the interruption. Then he told us about being surrounded with sincere souls, that in the past he had a few devils. He said, "I asked Divine Mother why they had to come and Divine Mother answered, 'that was to test your love for me.'" "Now I have sincere ones around me. I have no time for others. Before," he added, "I was easy and lenient, but not now." I admired Guruji's opal stones cross (blue opals, very rare) and he said, "these are very rare blue opals which came to me after a vision from a friend who has the mine in Australia." Then he told us of the large ones he has and added, "you'll have to see them sometime." I reminded Guruji of seeing the collection in Encinitas and he said, "you will have to see these sometime, they are beautiful, but I'm not attached to them. I have nothing—no money in my name. I would give these opals away and think nothing of it. I need nothing and want nothing material, I just want true souls." Then he mentioned, "out of thousands who seek him, I really find him." I offered my services to Guruji saying, "if there is any-thing I can do to help you, please let me know." He gra-ciously bowed and thanked me very much for offering (to my soul). He again blessed us—we kissed his right hand, then he pressed our hand (individually to his right temple) and again asked God and Divine Mother to bless us. I felt and still feel God's Holy Vibrations throughout my spirit, soul, mind, and body. God has brought us together again on this earth to do His (God's) Holy, Divine work in this great time of need. God, we thank Thee for Thee and Thy Divine, Blessed Teachers and Disciples.

God Bless Everyone—Mary S. Peck

~

ADDENDUM E

WHY FEAR DEATH?

Why should I fear death
When I can meet God
And see family and friends?
They've gone ahead and wait
To greet me and hug and say:
"We're glad to see you again."

I can lay down this worn garment
Now rent from years of pain, chill winds,
Burning suns and unfilled dreams.
But gladness too … and on the way –
Completed duties.

I fear not to discard this cloak
For a new beginning.
Like emerging tulip bulbs
Come alive at spring's beckoning.
What beauty! What joy!

Think what I can do.

I'll write compelling stories,

Perhaps a poem or two.

Then a soft low whisper from behind:

"When here you're home.

You'll pass beyond the poet's pen –

You are the poem."

— David A. Stockton

⌘

ADDENDUM F

The Gathering Time
(written October 18, 1982)

The gathering time –
When parts of the Whole return
To be placed in the Crown Divine;
Count my soul—make it shine.

You've given me a part of You
That I nurture and grow;
Make it shine;
This gift of love … this soul of mine.

Not from the accolades of masses
Does my soul its growth impart.
But with the silent, enduring, pulling —
The tugging of Your heart.

Through the dimness of the earth.
And in the soul's dark depth;

The passing of all time and its new rebirth
That I may shine … that I may shine.

Care not for setting, sad regretting;
All will be Thine.
Angry tears, constant fears, can dull the shine;
Weary actions, dissatisfactions, are cured by time.

Hurting, salves of learning placed on my jewel
(That gift of Thine)
Rubbed by the world's grit and sands of time.
Refine my soul! Bring back the shine.

With ego gone and wanting ceased,
I return to You what was always Thine.
Home—at last—in deepest peace;
This soul of mine … at the gathering time.

— Mary Peck Stockton

The End